D1555367

UNIVERSAL LIMITED ART EDITIONS

Forty Years of Contemporary

PROOF POSITIVE

American Printmaking at ULAE

1957-1997

THE CORCORAN GALLERY OF ART, WASHINGTON, DC
DISTRIBUTED BY
HARRY N. ABRAMS, INC., PUBLISHERS

This catalogue is published on the occasion of the special exhibition *Proof Positive: Forty Years of Contemporary American Printmaking at ULAE, 1957-1997*, organized by The Corcoran Gallery of Art, Washington, DC in association with Universal Limited Art Editions, West Islip, New York. Unless otherwise noted, the works are lent by Universal Limited Art Editions. First Edition: February 1997, Second Edition: October 1997.

This exhibition and subsequent collection programs are generously supported by THE FRIENDS OF ULAE AT THE CORCORAN.

PUBLISHED BY THE CORCORAN GALLERY OF ART, WASHINGTON, DC
EXHIBITION DIRECTOR: *Jack Cowart*
GUEST CO-CURATOR: *Sue Scott*
CATALOGUE DESIGN: *Lisa Ratkus*
EDITOR: *Mary Yakush*
EXHIBITION ASSISTANTS: *Laura Coyle, Larissa Goldston*

The exhibition schedule, at time of publication:
The Corcoran Gallery of Art
Washington, District of Columbia
15 February-30 June 1997

Gallery of Contemporary Art
University of Colorado at Colorado Springs, Colorado
4 August-19 September 1997

UCLA at the Armand Hammer Museum of Art and Cultural Center
Los Angeles, California
27 October 1997-4 January 1998

Sezon Museum of Art
Tokyo, Japan
27 February-6 April 1998

TABLE OF CONTENTS

Jack Cowart
Deputy Director & Chief Curator
The Corcoran Gallery of Art

The Atelier Press

The second half of our twentieth century has seen the commercial invention and professionalization of the atelier or studio press. Maurice and Tatyana Grosman, with caring, inspired help from friends and major artists, created one of the most effective and enduring of these American presses, which they ambitiously named Universal Limited Art Editions (ULAE). It's mission was to be an intimate facility dedicated to select artists and their progressive concepts, supported by talented master printers and the active engagement of Tatyana, the ultimate *propriétaire*. In the converted caretaker's cottage of a mid-Long Island Victorian estate, this press became a mecca, inspiring highly personalized and beautiful, if sometimes inherently impractical, small editions, fostering artist-poet collaborations, and producing some of the most important painterly and expressive prints and artists' books of our post-war period.

At the end of this century, when our frame of reference has already been shaped by the so-called 1960s print and 1970s photography "explosions," we are surprised to learn that at ULAE's first showings, the art establishment frequently dismissed contemporary prints as a popular but creatively inferior species. Critics willfully ignored the profound history of graphic arts, which pre-dated the Renaissance and extended into the modern era with the remarkable flowering of the European graphic age from Goya to Matisse, Munch and Picasso, and the many American late nineteenth-and early twentieth-century etching and art lithography revivals. Thus, in the mid-1950s ULAE and a handful of other small atelier presses had to re-validate contemporary independent American printmaking.

The atelier or studio press is a wondrous thing. At its best, it is a place where artistic and technical risks can be taken, privately and with a fullness of time for reflection and creative adjustment. Such a press is not about mass-production or delegation. Each decision is a personal one with its evident consequences. Some of the greatest artist/printmakers have kept presses in their own studios and they have often invited peers to use the equipment. Other artists have depended on university or commercial printmaking shops. ULAE evolved as a hybrid of these two. It became a semi-private artistic press with a distinctive creative atmosphere allowing a hand-selected group of artists to share facilities and expertise to meet the challenges of making new art – - with perhaps just enough production to pay the monthly bills.

My own first graphics exhibition, now twenty-three years ago, was the initial comprehensive display of prints from The Untitled Press, Robert Rauschenberg's Captiva, Florida, studio press. Untitled's first press was installed by Bill Goldston, then a printer at ULAE, and Bob Petersen, formerly a printer at Gemini, G.E.L., Los Angeles. They were responding to Rauschenberg's need for a working tool to expand, at his home, the processes and vision he was developing at ULAE. For a number of years, Rauschenberg invited other artists to visit, work, and collaborate in Captiva.

By the early 1980s, however, the generous ideals of ULAE and its equivalents spawned dozens more presses and graphic centers. The American printmaking community expanded to comprise multiple university printmaking facilities, major commercial shops, exquisite individual specialty presses, and a host of options in between. These have found numerous expressive variants and range widely in production size, technological emphasis, executive and master printer personality, geographic location, and commercial expertise. Now, more than ever before, almost any contemporary artist can have access to a remarkable array of exciting printmaking options.

GENERATIONAL CRISIS

Driving across Long Island one day, his mind freed by the routine commute, Bill Goldston worries, saying, "You see, that's the problem...we have a generational crisis." I interpret this as follows. In the early days of ULAE, with the artist Maurice Grosman as the sensitive talent scout and with the particular creative engagements of Tatyana as ULAE's muse in a smaller New York artworld with a visible number of enthusiastic supporters, the roster of then-young and emerging artists appears to have had a certain inevitability. Its apparent obviousness is enhanced today because this early generation has retained so much critical value. After forty years, Jasper Johns, Robert Rauschenberg, Jim Dine, James Rosenquist, Barnett Newman, Robert Motherwell, Helen Frankenthaler, Grace Hartigan, Cy Twombly, Marisol, and Larry Rivers, among others, have all left deep and lasting marks on contemporary art history. Several of these masters continue to produce remarkable works at this press, creating a curious generational time-warp. How, then, can today's ULAE avoid self-consciousness and break with its own illustrious history as it pursues its own necessary creative risks?

This ULAE "generational crisis" is how to find ways to accompany and encourage the next generations as they forge artistic and creative change. It cannot be by mere technological wizardry or the "Art" part can get lost. It cannot be by returning to indulged pleasures of the elegant, virtuosic form. It is not by the standard revolutionary patricide of a full, bloody revolt against the elders. Instead, the new generations of ULAE need to find their own new edges, to push art beyond its shared history. Each of the younger artists working at West Islip knows about their celebrated predecessors at ULAE. They know the history of the American studio print revolution and they know the intricate end-games of the avant-guard artists and critics that seem so at odds with the creation of the discrete, perfect and beautiful object. They know that their very beginning point in printmaking has to challenge the high achievement of the elder generation. The new generations have to exceed just to be equal. They have to do much more to be judged better. It is a tremendous assumption of responsibility.

AN EXHIBITION

This current celebratory exhibition is a triumph of enthusiastic forgiveness over disappointment. The Corcoran and ULAE had planned an exhibition to mark the shop's anniversary, its fifteenth, in 1972. Major works were conceived and hopes were raised, but that exhibition was not to be. Happily, for our nation's capital and the rest of our tour venues, for the Corcoran museum and school of art and its current staff, and for even the longer and more distinguished history of ULAE, we have saved the best for now: the fortieth anniversary in 1997. As an added bonus, we can now see more clearly the twenty-five so-called Grosman years, fifteen of the so-called Goldston years, and even an intimation of what the coming years will hold. At the Corcoran we leapt at the chance to organize this exhibition, catalogue, and world tour. We feel privileged that Bill Goldston and all those at the shop, plus the artists and the guest co-curator Sue Scott, sought us out. We know that the grand and noble spaces of the Corcoran Gallery beckoned to Tatyana Grosman in the 1970s. We feel certain that this current exhibition in those same fine galleries, now as the first comprehensive retrospective of ULAE's forty years, will supremely satisfy and close the circuit left so open over these intervening twenty-five years.

There have been thirty-five artists who have worked at ULAE since its founding and they have produced 632 editions from 1957 to January 1997. The acquisition of the Grosman ULAE archives by The Art Institute of Chicago in 1982 produced an extremely useful catalogue raisonné of all the shop's editions from 1957 to 1982. Our current catalogue is focused on the choice Corcoran exhibition, which even still comprises more than 180 of ULAE's most distinguished editions. The next project to evolve from this Corcoran exhibition may very well be the creation of a complementary electronic catalogue of ULAE's more than 213 editions issued since 1982.

It is not feasible to display every work by every artist who has worked at ULAE. Therefore we have made certain aesthetic and strategic selections. In our curatorial dialogues, we took care to balance the historic icons of the early years of the shop and the inventive, energetic production of the present. Many great and well-known works could not be included, the better to leave space for a fresh view of other major works and the new work of younger artists. ULAE is a living and very human organism and this survey exhibition and catalogue strive to find that perfect point between history and the exciting present/future.

ACKNOWLEDGEMENTS
Profound thanks are due Bill Goldston and Larissa Goldston for their generosity, tireless dedication, and truly infectious energies on behalf of this project over the last five years. They are a great father-daughter team and they have been unstinting in their persuasive negotiations, critical information, editorial support, photography, research, and preparations for this exhibition and catalogue. Thanks also to the guest co-curator Sue Scott who, with Bill Goldston, expanded her earlier ULAE proposal destined for another place and time and then worked so effectively to initiate this Corcoran international celebration. We owe a very special recognition to poet Tony Towle. His eye-witness account and engaging powers of expression have given us a rare, vivid picture of the early days of this shop that Tatyana and Maurice built. We feel especially privileged that he would share his previously unpublished memoirs with us and we thank him also for his added editorial advice.

The artists, printers, and preparators who have worked at ULAE have been extremely generous with their recollections, energies and information. Without them, the history and the art, of course, would not have been possible. We offer this exhibition as testimony to their artistic achievements and we delight in sharing their visual discoveries and the beauty of their printed work. We especially thank the generous private lenders to this traveling exhibition and take pleasure in listing them following this essay. Many have been long-time supporters of ULAE and we admire their complete dedication to our cause.

At the Corcoran, particular thanks is owed my exhibition research assistant Laura Coyle. Ms. Coyle previously improved a number of my prior complex exhibitions at the National Gallery of Art, and I was greatly relieved to find that she could arrive here in time to work an equal wonder with my ULAE enterprise. Thanks also to our graphic design director Lisa Ratkus, who has shaped a mountain of material into this most handsome publication, and in record time. We acknowledge the following Corcoran staff members for their essential efforts on behalf this exhibition: David C. Levy, President & Director; Michael J. Dunn, Vice President for Finance and Administration; Samuel Hoi, Dean of the Corcoran School of Art; Katy Ahmed, Director of Special Events; Steve Brown, Operations Manager; Cindy Rom, Registrar; Kirsten Verdi, Assistant Registrar; Elizabeth Parr, Assistant to the Deputy Director; Clyde Paton, Preparator; Greg Angelone, Assistant Preparator; Ken Ashton, Museum Technician; and Jan Rothschild, Director of Public Relations. In Washington, we have benefited from the formidable professional editing talents and stoic patience of Mary Yakush. She took our cause to heart and has helped us craft a most useful commemorative publication. We also thank the multi-talented Christopher French, who is both an artist and an editor, for his work on the artists' biographies.

I wish to recognize Riva Castleman and David Kiehl for their most generous personal counsel and professional courtesies. They have been important points of reference and support when we have needed them, and their advice has always been enthusiastically and selflessly offered.

This exhibition has a complex and ambitious touring schedule and we thank those museums and their staffs who are currently participating in this international project:
Gallery of Contemporary Art, University of Colorado, Colorado Springs – Gerry Riggs, Director; UCLA at The Armand Hammer Museum of Art and Cultural Center, Los Angeles – Henry T. Hopkins, Director and Cindy Burlingham, Acting Chief Curator; Sezon Museum of Art, Tokyo – Makito Hayashi, Deputy Director and Hisako Tsuchida, Curator. And we look forward to forming additional partnerships as our exhibition continues its tour of the Asian Pacific and Europe.

This exhibition and subsequent collection programs are generously supported by a new group: THE FRIENDS OF ULAE AT THE CORCORAN. We look forward to many years of nurturing and expanding this national patrons' consortium to the significant benefit of our institution's print department and its contemporary acquisition, display, and reference projects.

Finally, this catalogue would not have been possible without the profound financial generosity of Emily Fisher Landau. We are delighted with this very special patronage made on behalf of her long support and very caring association with ULAE.

DOUG AND CATHLEEN BENNETT

LAURA BURROWS-JACKSON

LEO CASTELLI

NANCY AND TOM DRISCOLL

ROBERT AND BRENDA EDELSON

THE FEARER FAMILY

DR. AND MRS. ROBERT FELDMAN

JO FIELDER

HELEN FRANKENTHALER

TONY AND GAIL GANZ

BRIAN GOLDSTON

RENIE AND STAN HELFGOTT

JASPER JOHNS

MR. AND MRS. DENNIS KANNENBERG

JOHN AND CHRISTINA LUND

ROBERT AND JANE MEYERHOFF

NATIONAL GALLERY OF ART

PETER AND SUSAN RALSTON

CAROL AND MORTON RAPP

ROBERT RAUSCHENBERG

LARRY RIVERS

JANE FEARER SAFER

LORENA AND JAMES SALCEDO-WATSON

THE SCHWEBER FAMILY

SCOTT SMITH

MR. AND MRS. SHELDON SOFFER

UNIVERSAL LIMITED ART EDITIONS

DOUGLAS AND LESLIE VOLLE

BRUCE AND MARLENE WANKEL

CRAIG AND LISA ZAMMIELLO

AND THOSE WHO CHOOSE TO REMAIN ANONYMOUS

Tony Towle

I first traveled to Tatyana Grosman's Universal Limited Art Editions on June 24, 1964. It was a few minutes after 10 a.m. as the train approached Babylon station. I looked out the window and saw geese swimming on a lake through a mist. Then the mist cleared and there was traffic visible behind the lake, on Montauk Highway, with a typical brick high school coming into view as well. The moment of rural enchantment had already disintegrated by the time I got off the train into a welter of competing taxi drivers loudly soliciting my business. However, Maurice, Tanya's husband, had been waiting for me and impatiently led me to his car. He was irritated that the train was late and complained about it in his Eastern-European accented English as if it were somehow my fault. But on the phone Tanya had seemed offended when I said "I would just take a cab," and Maurice, though in his mid-sixties, had assigned himself the task of picking me up from the station (and carried it out with resolute determination, though it was often inconvenient for him, for many years).

I was making this trip because Tanya had hired me to be ULAE's "secretary."[1] She was oblivious to the fact that in American business terms a secretary was usually a woman that typed up dictated letters for an older (male) executive. For her, the typical "secretary" was poet Rainer Rilke, who for a time served as secretary to the sculptor Rodin. That I was a poet, in fact, was of importance to her. Poets were an integral part of the art scene Tanya knew in Europe. This connection between art and literature was also true of the circles in which I had recently become involved. It was exemplified by poet Frank O'Hara, who was also a curator at the Museum of Modern Art, a personal friend of many contemporary painters and

Maurice and Tatyana Grosman, 1960.

sculptors, and had become a friend (and something of a mentor) of mine, as well.

The reason Tanya felt she needed a full-time secretary was due to the recent show, *American Painters as New Lithographers*, organized by William S. Lieberman, curator of prints at the Museum of Modern Art. Although not a survey of lithographs from Universal per se, the only work in the show not printed at the studio was that of Sam Francis.[2] Tanya felt strongly that the prestige of being in an exhibition at MOMA was going to bring a great deal of new attention to the studio and she wanted to be prepared for the increased correspondence. Since it seemed only logical to her that a poet should answer letters relating to "her" artists, she sought advice from the only poet she knew personally: Frank O'Hara. Frank had been the collaborator with Larry Rivers on ULAE's first major project, the portfolio *Stones,* 1957-59.[3] Frank told her he knew of a young poet who needed a job. That was me. Tanya interviewed me briefly at Frank's loft in New York, decided that I would come out to West Islip four days a week (since as a poet I would also need time to write), but that these four days could vary according to what was going on at the studio. She gave me a check (Tanya was always very smart about giving money in advance to secure someone's services) and it was agreed that I would take the train from Penn Station that arrived in Babylon at 10 o'clock. I'm sure she wanted me to take an earlier train but I have never been a "morning person" and the 8:40 seemed plenty early enough. Tanya had retained a Russian accent that decades of French and German and English had not managed to supersede. It took some getting used to. She also had a somewhat deceptive motherly (or grandmotherly, depending on your age) quality, which made it seem that working at ULAE was going to be easy and pleasant. Frank knew Tanya had her idiosyncrasies, but he must have decided to let me discover that for myself.

It took about 15 minutes to drive east from the train station to the Robert Moses Causeway (used by thousands of people each summer to get to Captree State Park, on the western tip of Fire Island). Just past the Causeway, Maurice took a left, past a sizeable mansion on the corner, wound around a curve past suburban houses, took another left and pulled up on a short, dead-end street in front of the second of two houses on the right. This was 5 Skidmore Place, West Islip, Long Island, the ex-gardener's cottage on the former estate of the mansion we had just passed.[4]

To get to the house, one walked across a large front yard dominated by a towering catalpa tree, to the right of which was an extremely large forsythia bush (which, every April, bloomed into a mass of brilliant yellow). There was a sizeable rectangular stone table set up under the catalpa. The left side of the building was the original diminutive two-story Victorian cottage with a sharply peaked roof, to which a front porch had been added. There had also been the addition of a garage on the right side of this original structure, with a utility room above it but, by 1964, the garage had become the lithography studio and the room above it was where the prints were stored and shown.

On warm and sunny days, like this June 24th, the studio doors were open. I started to go into the house that way, where a young woman (Lee Bontecou) was standing over a large slab of stone, drawing on it. I committed the greatest faux-pas one could make at

5 SKIDMORE PLACE AND THE CATALPA TREE.

ULAE: disturbing an artist at work. Then, having gone into the "house" part of the house the proper way, through the front door, I found myself in the first of the three downstairs rooms: a small "reception" room facing the street, where there was a door to the studio. A slightly larger "sitting room" faced the back, from which one entered the much larger but low-ceilinged space that had a small kitchen at one end (the back) and a long glass-topped dining table set against the wall facing west toward the Causeway. Here I committed my second faux-pas of the day: since no one else was in the kitchen when I arrived, I took my cup of coffee and sat down at the short end of the table, facing the kitchen, in the spot reserved for the visiting artist![5]

Then, having drunk my coffee, I didn't really know what I was supposed to do in this overwhelmingly un-officelike setting. Tanya wasn't much help, for when an artist was working she was preoccupied with what was going on in the studio, making sure that he or she had everything needed, whether it be sending someone to the city to pick up particular art supplies, or to the bakery to find a favorite pastry.

The one thing Tanya did tell me on that first day was that I should start keeping a diary. What kind of a diary, I wanted to know. She didn't seem to be quite sure herself. I suggested that I would note the work that was going on in studio, which artist was working, who was visiting, and so on. What would go into most diaries, one's private thoughts and feelings, did not seem appropriate to include because it was being kept as a reference, and Tanya (or any interested party, really) could have access to it. I therefore tried to keep it notational and "impersonal." However, it turned out to be more cryptic than I had really intended. It seems that I succeeded so well in being *imp*ersonal that no one has ever been able to make much sense of these diaries but me!

Lunches at Universal became legendary. Twelve at the table was not unusual (but hardly a record) either in the kitchen or, weather permitting, in the yard under the catalpa tree. Invited guests (most often museum personnel, art dealers, collectors, writers), an artist who was working that day (Tanya never invited two artists to work at the same time), the printers, myself, and anybody else who was present for one reason or another, all ate

LUNCH IN THE YARD, 1972.

together. The lunches were like dinners. Lunch had originally begun to be the main meal of the day in the Grosman household in 1955, because Maurice had had a heart attack and his doctors had advised him not to eat heavily before bedtime.[6] However, Tanya had decided that the printers (lithography printing is strenuous) also needed adequate fortification in the middle of their working day. In 1964 Maurice usually prepared lunch. Later, a local woman, Lucy Softye, took over the cooking in addition to her bookkeeping duties. Eventually, ULAE employed a full-time professional chef.

LITHO STONES AT ULAE.

The artists and printers were as accessible at the lunch table as they were off limits in the studio. I had seen one of Bontecou's imposing canvas-and-metal sculptures at the New York State Theatre in Lincoln Center a few months before and I have to admit that I unthinkingly assumed that *Lee* Bontecou was a

man. I also got to talk to the printer, Zigmunds (Zig) Priede, who was just finishing his third year at ULAE as master printer and was about to leave to teach lithography at the University of Minnesota.[7] After lunch I was permitted to go into the studio, which was taken up with the lithography press and dozens of rectangular lithographic stones ranging from one to four feet long and two to four inches thick. When, a few years later, wooden shelves were built along the walls of the studio to hold them, the studio seemed like a library of oversized stone tablets.

It was decided that the sitting room next to the kitchen would be my office. An old typewriter sat on a table near the window, which looked out onto the combined suburban landscape of the Grosman's narrow back yard and the adjacent manicured lawn of the neighbors on the next street. I usually didn't have much time to appreciate the view, however. From originally not knowing what I was supposed to do, I ended up, at one time or another, doing almost everything that needed being done (except print or cook lunch). First, there was constant travel to and from New York on a bewildering variety of visits and errands. For many years a typical morning could begin with a hasty trip to New York as soon as I arrived and gulped down some coffee. Tanya and I would often drop Maurice off at one of the chess clubs (a game about which he was passionate) in Greenwich Village, and I would take over driving Tanya around for the day – perhaps to the Leo Castelli Gallery, to drop off impressions of a new edition (if it was one of the artists who showed in his gallery), or to André Emmerich, if it was a new work by Helen Frankenthaler. Or we might be going to show prints to a collector, such as Victor Ganz, whose office was on Fifth Avenue (and who possessed Jasper Johns' favorite Picasso painting, Jasper told me once). We might go to David Davis or Sam Flax to see if there were any new and interesting handmade papers that Tanya could use to inspire the artists to create new work. There was a constant series of trips to the craftspeople, mostly located in the city, that made the unique boxes and folders and portfolios for such works as Barnett Newman's *18 Cantos*, 1963-64; Bontecou's *Fifth Stone, Sixth Stone*, 1967-68; Fritz Glarner's *Recollection*, 1964-68; Larry Rivers and Terry Southern's *The Donkey and the Darling*, 1967-77; Edwin Schlossberg's *WORDSWORDSWORDS*, 1967-68; or R. Buckminster Fuller's *Tetrascroll*, 1975-77. Once, in 1966, I even had to carry three litho stones the six flights up to Larry Rivers' loft on East 14th Street (the elevator was out of order). Also, before Tanya regularly hired limousines for the purpose, I sometimes kept the car overnight to bring an artist or a collector or museum person back to West Islip the next morning.

There were actual "secretarial" duties as well: the correspondence Tanya was expecting did materialize; also billing, sending out biographies of the artists (which had to be typed up one copy at a time) and typing a "documentative description" (artist, number of stones, paper, size, etc.) on ULAE stationery for each print that went out of the studio. Since Tanya's concept of perfection did not permit erasures, these tasks could be quite time-consuming in themselves.

Tanya had other quirks, too. I was required always to wear a jacket and tie, no matter how hot it was. Visitors would remark on it, thinking it was *my* idea. She could be overly demanding, and seemingly irrational about inconsequential (to anyone else) matters, and make personal criticisms out of the blue. Occasionally she would insist on idiosyncratic definitions for common words: "momentum" to mean "moment" rather than "movement," for example. When I tried to explain that people took her meaning as the opposite of what she intended, she became irritated; it was not my place to correct her. On the other hand, she could be generous and caring, and in the long run had the best interests of her employees at heart.

In the early years, I occasionally served as a printer's assistant, sponging the litho stone between printings as it lay on the press, before the printer rolled it up with ink. (A litho stone needs to be kept wet so ink will stick only to the image, which has been "etched" into the stone, a delicate process that is a master printer's defining skill.) If the paper to be printed were large (say, 40" by 30"), it would take two people to place the paper exactly on top of the stone, so the image would print on the paper where it was supposed to. This registration was especially important if the final work had more than one element and so needed multiple printings that had to line up exactly. This precise placement of the paper was achieved through the simple but tricky device of pushing two straight pins through each sheet of paper at two predetermined points, and placing the paper over the stone so that the pinheads would come to rest on tiny corresponding holes put in the stone for the purpose. The stone was then run through the (motorized) press under tremendous pressure and the ink transferred to the paper. The resulting "impression" was the lithograph. There was always a sense of excitement when the first proof of a stone was printed, the artist and printer waiting to see the results "hot off the press." And Tanya, of course, if she did not happen to be present, was to be called to the studio to see the latest proof. Nothing was more important for her than to follow a work (and offer suggestions) as it was developing.

But what I did most often was help show the prints to prospective purchasers, museum curators and directors, gallery owners, and collectors (as well as other interested parties, such as writers, who were not going to buy anything but got the full showing nonetheless). Tanya thought it was extremely important that ULAE prints end up in important collections, preferably museums. She would not sell more than two prints from an edition to a dealer, even if it were the artist's own gallery. To run across a ULAE work being hawked like ordinary merchandise from some catalogue was, to her, like unexpectedly running across one of your children soliciting on a street corner. Tanya insisted on ULAE prints being treated with respect, for both the artists' sake and her own, as their publisher, and tried to exert a control over their existence, even long after they were sold from the studio. Many in the art world found this approach high-handed and meddlesome.

I certainly got to know the prints intimately. Aside from looking at a particular work the many times that we showed it, I soon was assisting Tanya in going through a new edition to select what would be the edition, separating those prints from the impressions that would be proofs, or might just be torn up by the artist and destroyed. These differences in the printing could be very slight, even minuscule, but it was important that the edition be as consistent as humanly possible.[8] Then came time for the artist to determine the size of the edition, sign and number the prints, designate the location of the publisher's seal, give the work a title, and decide on the price for which

THE ULAE SEAL.

each impression would be sold. Being on hand when a new work of art thus came to life was, often, to participate in a palpably magical moment.

Very early on, sealing the editions became another one of my duties. Anything printed at ULAE had to be embossed with the publisher's seal, which was the studio's logo. The artist's signature gave the work authenticity, the edition number (5/29, for example) gave it individual identity and showed how many there were, but the seal was necessary before the print had an official existence. It established the print's initial provenance.

The ULAE seal itself was a cumbersome cast-iron object that must have weighed at least ten pounds (or seemed to). Moreover, there wasn't very much variety in its placement because of the way it was made. The seal would only come out right side up if it were applied from the left side, and no further in than about seven inches from the edge of the paper. But, limited as this placement was, one still had to work a little by "feel" and it was important that the seal be embossed in the same place on each impression, exactly where the artist had designated.

BARNETT NEWMAN AND TATYANA GROSMAN, ULAE ETCHING STUDIO, 1968.

My first real test with its placement came that September (in 1964) when Tanya and I took the first portfolio of Newman's *18 Cantos* to the Newmans' apartment on West End Avenue to be signed and sealed.

If Tanya was deliberate, Newman could be even more so. He took a great deal of time thinking about every aspect of his work, and that included putting the publisher's seal on the *18 Cantos.* He wanted each lithograph of each portfolio to be sealed in his presence, as soon as he had signed it.[9] Newman's wife, Annalee, was always present, whether in West Islip or on West End Avenue. She was a traditional *femme de peintre,* an artist's wife. Their life together was unabashedly about his work.

Part of the "problem" with the seal here was the very essence of the effectiveness of the *Cantos* (and what made them essentially different from Newman's painting): the margins of the paper on which they were printed, some of which were extremely narrow. The artist had discovered, unexpectedly, that his images would be altered by these margins. (Newman talks about this in his "Preface" to the *18 Cantos.*) This is the kind of personal discovery Tanya was always hoping that the artists she invited to the studio would make.

Barney finally decided that I should emboss the seal diagonally, over his signature.[10] He said (half) jokingly that it would make the prints something like bank notes, that it would make it that much harder to forge his signature! Placing the seal this way wasn't always so easy, because it was not supposed to encroach on the image. That first attempt, with Tanya, Barney, and Annalee looking on, induced a lot of pressure indeed, and I don't think I was uniformly successful in getting the seal exactly where it was supposed to be.

After Tanya had decided to do original graphics, in 1957, on the advice of William Lieberman,[11] she found herself also influenced by Monroe Wheeler's *Modern Painters and Sculptors as Printmakers.* Tanya had come to the decision that she wanted to publish original books that were collaborations between artists and living poets or writers.[12] After an edition had sold out, it would be reproduced as a commercial book to be sold in museums. She thought that this secondary income, from the reproductions of the originals, would provide security for her and Maurice in their old age.

FRANK O'HARA (LEFT) AND
LARRY RIVERS (RIGHT)
WORKING ON THE PORTFOLIO
STONES IN RIVERS' SECOND
AVENUE STUDIO. 1958.

TATYANA GROSMAN AND LARRY
RIVERS, ULAE ETCHING
STUDIO. 1967.

The Grosmans had met Larry Rivers on a ship to Europe in 1950, so Tanya approached him first. Frank O'Hara was at Larry's house in Southampton (in eastern Long Island) when Tanya broached the idea, and *Stones* was the eventual result. Certain characteristics typical of many ULAE books and portfolios were embodied in *Stones*, such as paper commissioned especially for the edition (in this case by a Long Island paper maker named Douglass Howell), and a "binding" reflecting some aspect relating to the contents. Since Frank and Larry always seemed to be wearing blue jeans when they worked, the folder was bound in denim. Tanya's recollection was that sometimes, while Larry was waiting for Frank to show up so they could work together on one of the *Stones,* he did drawings on other stones that were not related to the book. This is how ULAE came to publish single editions as well as portfolios.

Two of Larry's early single editions were the two variations of *Ford Chassis,* 1961. The second differs from the first in having the Hebrew letters for "kosher" added. The artist was ironically amused when he learned that a member of the Ford family had bought one of these through Gertrude Kasle, ULAE's gallery representative in Detroit, as Henry Ford himself was known to have been notoriously anti-Semitic.

Larry did a lot of "cutout" work in his studio. For years he pushed Tanya to publish a three-dimensional lithograph of some sort, which she resisted on the grounds that she didn't quite see how it could be accomplished technically. When Larry did a portrait of his friend

Diane, and it turned out that the stone was going to be printed as a "regular" two-dimensional lithograph, he insisted that it be titled *Diane Raised I*, 1970. There came to be a *Diane Raised II*, 1970-71; *III*, 1970-71; and *IV*, 1970-74, version *III* having some collage, but not what the artist had in mind. *Diana with Poem*, 1970-74 is really *Diane Raised V*, and the only version that is really "raised." Tanya had given Bill Goldston's children some pop-up books for Christmas, which inspired the technical solution. Larry originally wanted to add his own text. He asked me to look up all the meanings of and references to "Diane" and "Diana." This wasn't satisfactory, and eventually the poet Kenneth Koch, a long-time friend of Larry's (and mine) supplied a poem. The work is one of the rare single-edition works (as opposed to books and portfolios) from ULAE that includes collaborative writing.

Larry's collaboration with writer Terry Southern on the book *The Donkey and the Darling* took ten years to come to fruition, a little long even by ULAE's leisurely standards.[13] Part of this was due to the length of the text. It was a whole short story, a fairy tale, which Terry had written for his son, Nile, although it is filled with (very funny) adult satire as well as being true to its genre. Larry went with the allegorical possibilities of Terry's characters (Thin Wisdom is a book reading himself) and brought in some modern symbolism as well (Bad Witch is a hypodermic needle). Larry told me in an unpublished interview that he had a long list of the names of the story's characters pinned up in his studio for "a very long time."[14] Even when Larry had created the main characters, it could be seen that if the entire book was done as elaborately, with as many printings as the first eight pages, the enterprise would take virtually forever. (The book is 52 pages as it is.) The answer here was to continue the tale with Larry creating mostly artistic "vignettes" of the text and treating the over-the-top Arabian Nights-style typeface as art in itself. Larry sometimes used the type to follow the text literally, as the eponymous Donkey "prancing" on page 27.

Jasper Johns, whom Tanya invited to ULAE in 1960, seemed to understand from his first introduction to the medium what made lithography different, as a work on paper, from his drawings, and it seemed to suit his artistic sensibility. In lithography, you could change the image by printing another stone over it, see how it looked, and if you decided against the addition you could "subtract" it and still have the original by simply printing the first stone by itself. This was the case with Jasper's first released edition in 1960, *Target*. A second "wash" stone was tried and then rejected.[15] Or one could keep adding elements (stones) until you had what you wanted (although just a touch of additional color would mean the same amount of work for the printer: one more pass through the press for the entire edition). *False Start I*, 1962, was composed of eleven stones in a variety of colors. A lithographic stone is always printed first in black, so everything in the image can be seen clearly. Afterwards, however, the stones can be printed, successively, in any number of different colors, and on different papers as well, creating a new work each time. With an economy of means impossible in drawing or painting, the litho stones used for *False Start I* were then in 1962 printed as *False Start II* in ten shades of gray and one subtle touch of violet in the lower right corner. In the same year, *Painting with Two Balls I* (in red, yellow, and blue) was printed in shades of gray as *II* with two of the three elements of the first version being utilized.

In addition, Jasper also made use of the *metamorphic* aspect of lithography, the fact that the image on the stone could be printed, altered, and then printed again. The three variations of *Flag*, 1960, are illustrations of this, but the possibilities are brilliantly exemplified by the three portfolios, *0-9*, 1960-63. Among the very first stones that Jasper did was a large "0," with the complete sequence of miniature numerals "0" through "9" in two rows, above it. He had an idea for a ten-lithograph sequence in which, after the "0" was printed, the image would be modified into a "1," and so on through "9." At first Tanya wasn't quite sure what the artist meant, but she was sure that a project this complex and interesting called for special paper. Eventually (probably in 1962), she ordered three different types of paper (for what was now going to be three variations on the theme) from the Angoumois

mills in France. While the paper for Larry and Frank's *Stones* was also handmade for the occasion, the papers for *0-9* had the elegant added feature of the artist's signature as their watermark.

The "0" stone was etched and a few proofs pulled by Robert Blackburn in 1960[16] but, due to the wait for the paper, the editions weren't printed until 1963, by Zig Priede. The procedure was that the "0" would be printed in all three editions (with ten portfolios in each of the three: *A/C*: in black on off-white paper; *B/C*: in gray on unbleached paper; and *C/C*: in colors on white). Jasper would then rework the "0" into a "1" and that numeral would be printed, and so forth, until the "9" of *C/C*, which was in white on white, the "diminuendo," as Tanya liked to call it, which brought the series to a logical close. Also, Jasper made an "overprint" stone for each of the numerals, which corresponded to that number in the edition. The overprint "6" would be printed on 6/10 *A/C, B/C*, and *C/C*, for example. Zig printed each numeral of *B/C* first, because the gray ink on the unbleached paper was the trickiest to get right. It is for this reason that the "0" of the *B/C* portfolio, as the very first print of the set, was dated '60 by the artist, while the rest of the lithographs in the editions were dated '63. Needless to say, there was a certain risk involved in this project since, if the stone broke (or if Priede somehow fouled up in etching one of the images) at, say, the number "5," then the whole project would have been in jeopardy.

In 1971, Johns had occasion to take advantage of a different kind of lithographic opportunity. He was the first artist to make use of a new lithography press ULAE had recently purchased. It was a handfed offset proofing press, whose function was to provide a "perfect proof" on a photo plate that was then used for long-run offset editions (such as reproductions in books and magazines). Tanya (and Bill Goldston, who had recently arrived from Minneapolis but was already beginning to have an influence on technical decisions) thought that this instrument would be extremely valuable for having control over the quality of the reproductions for a projected catalogue raisonné of the studio's production.[17]

This press was moved into a new building in the nearby town of Bay Shore in June.[18] At some point Jasper had asked if hand-drawn litho plates could be printed on the press, as well as photo plates. The commercially trained printer, James V. (Jim) Smith, who came over to ULAE with the press when it was purchased, simply didn't know, no one had ever tried it. It turned out that hand-drawn plates worked beautifully and *Decoy,* 1971, was the proof. One feature of this new press that made it different from the traditional litho press was that it had a "light touch." This encouraged multiple printings as there was little stress on the paper (as opposed to the intense pressure needed by the hand press to pick up the ink from the stone), and Jasper ended by adding 18 plates to the black "leg" image with wash that had been printed on a large stone in the West Islip studio.[19] *Decoy II,* 1971–73, had seven more added to that, for a total of 26 printings. When Tanya asked Jasper about the punched hole in *Decoy* that broke the spectrum line at the bottom of the print, he answered with cryptic humor that it was "a way out." Tanya didn't hear the "a" and thought he said that it was "way out," as in a variation of the expression "Far out!" She would repeat this "insight" to everyone we showed the print to, but this was a case of where I didn't feel disloyal in letting

MAURICE GROSMAN (LEFT) AND ROBERT RAUSCHENBERG (RIGHT), ULAE STUDIO, C. 1962-64.

the listener know, when Tanya was not present, what the artist had actually said.

Robert Rauschenberg, when he first came to the studio in 1962, primarily employed the "classic" print format of black image on white paper, but with a contemporary iconography taken from current events just passed: discarded printers' mattes and plates he picked up from *The New York Times* and *The Herald Tribune.* Bob inked these and applied them directly to litho stones in different combinations, augmented with abstract drawing and wash, and achieved a great variety of effects in more than a dozen lithographs from 1962 to 1964.[20]

Lithographic stones could exhibit their own version of mortality. *License,* 1962, was an edition of only 16 because the stone broke while being printed. The following year, while being proofed, another large stone of Rauschenberg's cracked under the pressure of the press. One of Tanya's favorite stories was recounting how Bob had turned this misadventure into triumph. He directed that the broken stone be printed anyway, with its ever-widening crack separating the two pieces. He then made a small second stone, a drawing of the debris from the crack, as if it had fallen down the opening to the bottom of the paper. Fittingly, he titled it *Accident,* 1963, and it won the Grand Prize at the Ljubljana (Yugoslavia) international print biennial, at the time the most prestigious print exposition in the world. Losing large stones was a high price to pay, however, even for international recognition. But, in 1964, it happened yet again. The stone of *Breakthrough I,* 1964, cracked too and the edition was stopped at 20.[21] The following year, Bob created *Breakthrough II,* 1965, by adding three stones, but the head of the Statue of Liberty (at the top of the print) crumbled further with each pass through the press. This was just allowed to happen, so each succeeding impression carried less and less of this image. Finally the stone just crumbled away.[22]

JIM DINE WORKING ON *A HEART AT THE OPERA*, ULAE STUDIO, 1983.

It was always a party when Bob came out to the studio. He often arrived late in the afternoon, with a bevy of friends/visitors/people who worked for him. Lavish food and drink would be set out (Maurice traditionally cooked lobsters for everyone on these occasions) and it was not unusual for Bob to be in the studio until three or four in the morning. Tanya would then have a local limousine service take everybody back to the city. (This often included me, as I continued to live in New York and commute.)

Jim Dine had been brought out to ULAE in 1962 by Jasper Johns. In a catalogue piece for the ULAE works in his print retrospective of 1970, I quoted Jim as saying, "Tanya Grosman has been the catalyst for everything. She has made me aware of paper."[23] He was at the studio a number of times in the fall of 1964. I remember going into the studio one morning (it was not off-limits if an artist was not working in it) and being struck by the bold simplicity of the primary stone for *Eleven Part Self Portrait (Red Pony)*, 1964-65. Why the "Red Pony"? I asked the artist, just out of curiosity. Jim said, in effect, that he thought it seemed just naturally to be part of the title. I remember him including a quizzical look to the effect that I, as a poet, should be the last person to question this kind of oblique association.

Boot Silhouettes, 1965, was even simpler and bolder. The boots themselves (as I remember) were those the artist wore for a performance piece in England. Tanya wasn't too sure about this image. Probably the militaristic associations had something to do with it, although she did not describe her hesitation from that perspective. I believe her reservations were the reason the edition was only 20 (the paper, Rives BFK, was readily available). The public, however, had no such qualms, and the edition sold out quickly.

Dine's intuitive quickness on two occasions led him to add elements from the immediate environment at the spur of the moment, specifically from the kitchen: he put lithographic ink on half of an apple he had been eating, applied it to a stone, and it became an element of *Double Apple Palette with Gingham*, 1965. And one morning in 1972, while working on a large "heart diptych," Jim brought a French cruller from the kitchen into the studio, inked it up, and placed it on a large stone "where it needed something." This comestible also found its way into the title; however the artist decided on *2 Hearts (the Donut)*, 1970-72, knowing that "cruller" would not have had the same resonance.

James Rosenquist was one of the very few artists who had not already begun working at Universal by the time I started. Sometime in September of 1964, Maurice and Tanya had brought a few stones to the artist's Bowery studio in New York so he could get the feel of the medium in his own surroundings, before working more "publicly" with the printers. (This option was always offered to an artist that was invited to ULAE.) It was something of a party when Jim came out, too, though he was most often by himself, instead of with an entourage, like Rauschenberg. He was enthusiastic and cheerful and would sometimes bring expensive bottles of liquor for me and the printers (which Tanya somewhat disapproved of) and always had a store of the most delightfully non-sequitur anecdotes I have ever heard. However, Jim was very serious when it came to work, and would spend hours getting a stone just right. *Campaign*, 1965, was the first edition released, and it successfully compressed the artist's outsized "billboard" pop imagery into a mere 29-by-22-inch format. Jim's breakthrough came when he found the traditional litho crayons unsatisfactory and brought along his airbrush. By spraying tusche (lithographic ink) onto the stone (and sometimes using stencil, like the flower pattern in *Campaign*) he achieved some wonderfully delicate effects.

JAMES ROSENQUIST AND DONN STEWARD, WORKING ON *EXPO 67 MURAL-FIREPOLE 33' X 17'*, ULAE STUDIO 1967.

Occasionally a stone didn't actually have to break to become unusable. For reasons inexplicable to Tanya and more than one printer, one of the background stones for *Circles of Confusion*, 1965-66, would just not hold the image. Jim had put a lot of work into this print and, since it ended up being only an edition of 12, added the numeral 1, to indicate there would be a second version in the future (although it never happened).

Tanya usually tried to discourage the artists from doing a lithograph specifically after a drawing or painting (thinking that it was somehow "impure" or not treating the medium as if it required an independent effort of sensibility). However *Expo 67 Mural - Firepole 33' x 17'*, 1967, refers directly to the mural Rosenquist painted for the World's Fair held in Montreal.[24] The image was translated on six stones in a scale of exactly one inch to one foot. However, there was a technical

MARISOL, ULAE STUDIO, c.1970.

problem that had to be overcome, because the wide "blended" roll of the red and yellow ink together of the background (also creating orange) was very difficult to print consistently, with the colors tending to fuse too completely into each other.

One of the first evenings that Jim worked late, Maurice suggested (or, rather, directed) that I go back to the city with him in his truck to make sure he wouldn't get lost. As it happened, we were talking when we got to the point on the Southern State Parkway where one needed to take a right to get up to the Long Island Expressway. Instead, we ended up taking a leisurely two hours around Brooklyn on the Belt Parkway. Jim was very good-humored and forgiving, but I certainly heard about it from Maurice and Tanya. I never missed that turnoff again.

Marisol also received stones in her studio to experiment with in late August or early September 1964. As in her drawings, she utilized her own body as subject matter, in effects that could be whimsical, enigmatic, "dark," or all three together. In 1973, the artist created a number of works to augment a print retrospective to be held later that year at the New York Cultural Center, in Columbus Circle. One of these was *Catalpa Maiden About to Touch Herself*, in which she cast herself as a mysterious legend relating to the imposing shade tree in the front yard. Marisol picked leaves from the catalpa, inked them, pressed them on the stone, and added drawing. In *Diptych*, 1971, she put her whole body, unclothed and inked, on two large stones that, when printed, presented a rather frightening eight-foot self-portrait. (Tanya was very concerned for the artist's modesty during this procedure; she covered the glass doors of the studio with heavy paper and stood by the inside studio door to ensure no one could walk in on the artist inadvertently.)

Fritz Glarner's *Recollection*, 1964-68, was intended to be a lithographic recapitulation of an entire career (he had developed a style he termed Relational Painting). The artist had completed more than 50 stones for the project in 1964 and '65, most of which were printed by Ben Berns, the master printer at the time. He and Fritz (who was Swiss) had a particularly good rapport, partly because Ben (who was Dutch) was trained in Europe. *Recollection* was to be ready for Fritz to finalize when he and his wife, Lucie, returned from a trip to Europe in the spring of 1966. Fritz didn't like to fly because it was too dangerous, but their ship was hit by a violent storm in the Atlantic. (Lucie told me the waves were higher than the ship.) Fritz was knocked down and struck his head and taken off the ship to the hospital by helicopter.

He never fully recovered and remained partially paralyzed for the remaining six years of his life. Nonetheless, from his hospital bed he was able to write the text for the two stones that completed the project.[25] His mind must have wandered, but it was miraculous that he could still write on stones at all.[26] When it came time to sign the edition, in 1968, Fritz, though confined to a wheelchair, had gained total con-

Fritz Glarner signing *Recollection* with Tony Towle at the artist's studio, Huntington, Long Island, 1968.

Helen Frankenthaler, ULAE studio, 1964.

trol over his right hand so that his signatures – on almost 600 prints that needed to be signed, numbered and dated – possessed none of the tentativeness of the two text stones mentioned above. However, tragically *Recollection* was the last major work Glarner could accomplish by himself. As part of his practice in Relational Painting, the artist had pared down his palette to the primary colors of red, yellow, and blue, plus black and shades of gray. A curious feature of *Recollection* is that he used ocher and violet on several of the pages, as well.

Helen Frankenthaler brought her spontaneous, gestural sensibility to a medium whose nature makes an artist wait to see the results. Decisions on adding stones to the first image (or not), after it is printed, proofing the image in various colors, selecting the right paper on which to print, for example, are all time-consuming. As sometimes happened, Tanya would have a particular artist in mind for a particular paper, and this was the case with a batch of unbleached (brown) sheets she had brought back from the Angoumois mills in France with Helen's work in mind.[27] At first the artist was not impressed, but then thought, "My God, that's just like a slice of the stone itself! "[28]

It is fitting that there will finally be a ULAE exhibition under the auspices of the Corcoran Gallery of Art. In a diary entry dated May 12, 1969, I recorded that a curator from the Corcoran, Renato Danese, came out to discuss a ULAE retrospective that was intended to take place in the autumn of 1970. Plans for this exhibition, postponed time and again by new personnel, were not totally abandoned until several years later. However, during the course of the discussions Tanya paid a visit to the Corcoran Gallery. She took note of the very high ceilings of the exhibition space and felt that many of the prints might just "get lost" in it. She had the idea that each of the artists should create a "monumental" print.

Helen was the first to take advantage of this suggestion and asked for three large stones in order to create a triptych. Tanya had assumed that this "triptych" would be horizontal but recalled that Helen told her she wanted to make her gesture vertically. *Lot's Wife,* 1970-71, is indeed a triptych but the three sections overlap and are meant to be framed as one. Though *Lot's Wife* wears its scale lightly, at almost eleven feet it is certainly monumental! Most private collectors did not have ceilings high enough to hang it, and just showing it in the confines of the studio was somewhat of a production.

Other prints that were intended to have been seen in the Corcoran long before now are Motherwell's *Samurai,* 1971; Dine's *2 Hearts (the Donut),* 1970-72; Marisol's *Diptych,* 1971; and James Rosenquist's *Off the Continental Divide,* 1973-74 (which was printed on the handfed offset proofing press described above and used no less than 29 plates). By the time this work, and Rauschenberg's *Kitty Hawk,* 1974, were completed, the original Corcoran project had been abandoned.

Another project that ran out of time was the projected "15 Years" celebra-

LEFT TO RIGHT: ROBERT
RAUSCHENBERG, BILL GOLDSTON,
TATYANA GROSMAN, FRANK AKERS,
ZIGMUNDS PRIEDE AND MARION
JAVITS, ULAE STUDIO,
SUMMER 1969.

LEE BONTECOU WITH PROOF OF
SIXTH STONE I ON THE TABLE AND
FIFTH STONE ON THE WALL,
ULAE STUDIO, 1964.

tion (1957-72) of ULAE, and a special seal was created to identify these prints. When Jim Rosenquist's *15 Years Through a Drop of Water* was completed, it was already 1973; Edwin Schlossberg's *Fragments from a Place* was done in 1974, as was Bob Rauschenberg's *Tanya,* so by this time it was already a 17-year celebration.

Bob kept secret the fact that the subject of his commemorative lithograph was Tanya herself. I remember when he called us into the studio to see the first proofs. She was flattered and embarrassed in equal parts. To cover her self-consciousness, Bob pointed to the differentiation between the two brown stones that made up the image and said that he hoped we noticed how *completely different* the two colors were. (In fact, the two shades are so close that at first glance they look to be the same color.)

There was a misconception held by some in the art world that Tanya Grosman was only interested in "fancy" paper for ULAE prints. Her actual philosophy was not that the paper had to be fancy, but that it had to be right. The paper could certainly be exotic, however. One day, while Claes Oldenburg was working in the studio, Tanya received a letter from a Swiss gentleman named Fred Siegenthaler who, as a hobby, made paper himself, and during the course of his worldwide travels kept his eye out for unusual papers to send to ULAE. With this letter was a folded-up piece of paper that he stated he could obtain more of if Tanya were interested. Now don't laugh, the letter continued, but this is a sheet of hand-made Balinese toilet paper!

Tea Pot, 1975, was being proofed that day, and the Balinese paper was included as a possibility. The image simply looked the best on this paper, whatever its originally intended function.

It turned out that *Tea Pot* was the only completed edition that Oldenburg did at ULAE. Another artist who worked little, but notably, was Saul Steinberg. Those who know his work only from the photo-offset reproductions in *The New Yorker* will be surprised by the sensuous quality the lithographic stone gives to his drawing in *The Museum*, 1972, and *Main Street*, 1972-73.

In 1967, ULAE received a grant from the newly established National Endowment for the Arts to buy an etching press and introduce the artists to the possibilities of intaglio.[29] Lee Bontecou was one of the first artists to work in the newly established studio. Previously, when Tanya told me to keep a diary, she also urged me to "take notes" of Lee working on what became the three variations of *Sixth Stone*, 1964 (she had just finished *Fifth Stone* earlier in the year, which has a similar image). Tanya had some nebulous idea for a collaborative project in the future. Over the next three years, this included a semi-commercial book reproducing the lithographs with my notes, and a portfolio of small lithographs. Also over the three-year period, my notes had been whittled down into a relatively short descriptive piece. This became the facing text for the etchings

CLAES OLDENBURG, ULAE STUDIO, 1975.

ROBERT MOTHERWELL AND TATYANA GROSMAN, ULAE ETCHING STUDIO, NOVEMBER 1969.

R. BUCKMINSTER FULLER WITH *TETRASCROLL*, 1977.

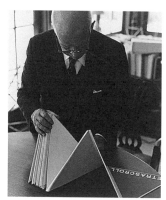

of the portfolio *Fifth Stone, Sixth Stone,* which Lee did to recall her lithographs of 1964. I wrote a poem as a kind of coda for the work. The box that contains the pages was bound in Indian Head, a type of cloth Lee often used for drawings with soot.

Soon after the etching studio was in operation, Cy Twombly happened to be visiting Rauschenberg in New York (August of 1967) and Bob brought him along to West Islip. Cy came out several more times in August and September, sometimes with Bob and later with Jasper, as well, who was also an old friend. While Bob (or Jasper) was working in the lithography studio, Twombly worked on intaglio plates in the "etching basement" as we came to refer to it, with Donn Steward.[30] The four *Notes*, 1967, were signed at the beginning of October, but the two large *Untitled* prints were not printed until 1974 (as Cy lived in Italy), and *Sketches*, begun in 1967, was released in 1975. As I noted in my diary at that time, these latter were the first plates Cy had worked on and he referred to them as "practice plates." Tanya told him there was no such thing.

The most elaborate etching portfolio done at ULAE, however, was Robert Motherwell's *A la pintura,* 1968-72, which was also the artist's magnum opus in a graphic medium. The artist and Steward had a good rapport, certainly preferable if not essential in any printer/artist collaboration that is going to take more than four years to complete.[31] Motherwell pretty much had to talk Tanya into this project, as the poem cycle by Spanish poet Rafael Alberti had already been published. The poet was still alive (and eventually paid a visit to the studio) but it was not the kind of direct and interactive collaboration that she preferred to see take place. However, she eventually agreed. The poems were an homage to color and Bob was a colorist. He also had a well-known affection and respect for Spanish art and culture (probably Motherwell's best-known paintings are the Spanish *Elegies*), which Tanya herself shared to a certain extent.

Jasper Johns brought Edwin Schlossberg out to visit (also in 1967), and within three months he was working on the "visual poems" that became *WORDSWORDSWORDS*, 1967-68. The poet used etching, lithography, and letter press in a variety of untraditional materials (such as Plexiglas and aluminum foil) that are an integral part of the poems themselves. "Each poem was conceived for the medium in which it was expressed," as he wrote in the Table of Contents/ Colophon page. Schlossberg introduced Tanya to R. Buckminster Fuller in 1975 on Fuller's eightieth birthday. The sensitivity of the lithographic stones was a revelation for Fuller, who had dealt mostly in the "practical" kinds of materials used for realizing his inventions, such as the geodesic dome, and in the nonmaterial realm of abstract ideas. *Tetrascroll* was a compendium of many of his ideas going back many decades. In fact, when "Bucky" (he insisted everyone call him this, though Tanya, typically,

EDWIN SCHLOSSBERG WITH PLATE OF
IN THE SHADOW FROM
WORDSWORDSWORDS, 1968.

ALEXANDER LIBERMAN, ULAE
STUDIO, 1977.

usually addressed him as "Dr. Fuller") started talking he always tended to include everything he knew, which was, to say the least, considerable. On several occasions, when *Tetrascroll*, 1975-77, was in progress, I would sit for hours typing up his notes while he was in the studio waiting for proofs. If Bob Rauschenberg stayed up late, Bucky could stay up all night! No one could keep up with this octogenarian. I had to bring in a friend of mine (another poet), Paul Violi, to take over some of the continuous typing duty.

It was perhaps appropriate that the last major portfolio project Tanya was fully involved with, *Nostalgia for the Present*, 1977-79, had a Russian theme.[32] It was a collaboration between the (relatively) young Soviet poet Andrei Voznesensky and Alexander Liberman, much older than Andrei and an émigré. Tanya had asked Voznesensky if the publicity surrounding his work at the studio would get him into trouble with the authorities back home. He replied that the more publicity he got the better off he was. The more he was written about in the West, the less likely the Soviet bureaucracy would be to act, for fear of embarrassing themselves with the outside world.

It can easily be seen that the books and portfolios that ULAE published are truly extraordinary works of art (as splendid and beautiful as so many of the single editions are). However the cost of producing them, the lavish care and virtually limitless expenditure that Tanya unhesitatingly bestowed on their production, had no correlation with the price that they could realistically command in the art market. Their singularity, as well as the actual number of prints the purchaser was getting for the money, made the books "best buys," in a way, yet they were often difficult to sell as well as uneconomical to produce. It seemed that American collectors, as sophisticated as they had become visually since, say, the 1950's, had not carried that refinement over into artistic/literary collaborations.

TONY TOWLE AND TATYANA GROSMAN ON THE FRONT PORCH, 5 SKIDMORE PLACE, EARLY 1970S.

Toward the end of summer every year there would usually come a moment in the yard at 5 Skidmore Place when a sudden breeze would rustle the tops of the trees in a premonition of autumn. I remember that Maurice's comment at such times to the effect that "the summer's over" had become a little more wistful each year. In February of 1976, Maurice passed away, twenty years after his life-threatening heart attack. Although Tanya had gone from being a *femme de peintre* in the 30's and 40's to an internationally recognized figure in the art world in her own right, she resisted anachronistic feminist interpretations of the success of her enterprise. While it is true that Maurice had less and less to do with the ULAE's actual operations, he was very much involved with the decisions Tanya made over the years. She certainly was not the same after his passing, for the last six years of her own life.

By the end of 1978 a number of complex personal problems dictated that I myself move on, although I was still involved in some of the studio's events and functions, and occasionally working there on a part-time basis, until 1981. Bill Goldston, who had become studio manager, was willing to put in the necessary hours and energy to maintain ULAE. Though Tanya could sometimes be difficult on a personal level, and there were many times over the years when I wondered why I was there, on some esthetic level we were in total agreement: art mattered. It was not just a "commodity." Through it all, I knew I was privileged to be a part of what was being created at Universal Limited Art Editions. I still think so today.

New York, June 1996

ENDNOTES

1 She had been introduced to me as "Tanya" but, very early on, when I offered to address her by the more formal "Tatyana," or even "Mrs. Grosman," she declined.

2 Francis, however, had worked on his first lithography stones with Tanya back in 1959, and she had been responsible for his interest in the medium. These stones were finally printed as editions and signed by the artist in 1968.

3 Tanya always insisted on an initial-by-initial pronunciation: U.L.A.E. and disliked hearing it pronounced as an acronym, such as YEW-LAY.

4 The extraordinary story of how Tanya and Maurice Grosman got to 5 Skidmore Place has been told in greatest detail by Calvin Tomkins, in *Off the Wall* (New York 1980), pp. 201-205 and in a shorter version by Amei Wallach, in *Universal Limited Art Editions* (Chicago and New York, 1989), pp.9-15.

5 Tanya decided, however, that it could be my spot if no artist were present that day.

6 It was in fact this unfortunate event that led Tanya to seek ways of creating a family income that eventually resulted in the founding of Universal Limited Art Editions.

7 Tanya tended to trust the expertise of Zig's students, and many came from the University of Minnesota to print at ULAE over the years, including Bill Goldston, who eventually became studio manager and, after Tanya's death, President of ULAE, and John A. Lund, master printer in lithography and later intaglio, from 1972 to 1996.

8 I remember in particular Tanya and my selecting the edition for Jasper's *Painting with a Ball*, in 1973, which comprised three shades of black. As close as the colors seemed at first, I was amazed by how apparent the differences became with continued scrutiny.

9 Most often the artist would designate the placement of the seal on one print and the edition would be sealed later.

10 Although he asked anyone, whatever the age difference, to call him "Barney," Tanya (even though they were born the same year) never called him anything but "Mr. Newman."

11 When Tanya had brought some of the silkscreens Maurice had done between 1955 and 1957 of work by Mary Callery and others (with their permission) to MOMA for possible sale, Lieberman had told her that they were very good but he couldn't consider buying them for the Museum because technically they were still "reproductions."

12 A great many of the well-known *livres de luxe* of the School of Paris were "collaborations" between living artists and past writers, such as Matisse illustrating the work of the 15th-century poet Charles d'Orléans.

13 Southern, who, sadly, recently passed away, is perhaps best known to the general public as the screenwriter of Stanley Kubrick's film, *Dr. Strangelove.*

14 June 24, 1977.

15 I had ample opportunity to contemplate Jasper's decision. On the wall in the ULAE "office," there hung a *Target* as printed, a proof of the wash stone, the two stones printed together, and a sketch of a *Target*, all in one frame.

16 Blackburn was ULAE's first professional printer, and worked there from 1957 to 1963. He went on to start his own workshop in New York.

17 Esthetic and technical control was everything at ULAE. In the matter of reproductions, commercial establishments could not be expected to lavish the time and care necessary to "get it right."

18 ULAE already had a letterpress in the Bay Shore building and it was being used primarily (by typesetter/printer Juda Rosenberg) for the Alberti poems in Robert Motherwell's *A la pintura*, 1968-72.

19 *Decoy* was originally intended to be *Passage III.*

20 Rauschenberg also created a "lithographic object," *Shades*, from 1964, with five (square) lithographs printed on Plexiglas that were rearrangeable within an aluminum frame (plus a stationary title, also on Plexiglas).

21 This "fault line" can be seen in Bontecou's *Fourth Stone*, which had been printed from the same stone the previous year.

22 It was decided that the "bed" of the press must have been uneven and that unequal pressure was breaking the stones; a new bed was made.

23 *Jim Dine: Complete Graphics*, (West Berlin 1970).

24 In its original site, the "fireman" was sliding down through an R. Buckminster Fuller geodesic dome.

25 Glarner had decided to collaborate with his own writings, as it were. If they had been previously published, then the text would be printed in type (type transferred to a litho stone), and if from his notebooks, he would write the text on stone by hand.

26 On the text stone for page 11, Glarner absent-mindedly wrote *New York...* twice, with three dots, not a comma, as in an address. He also put a French accent on the English *degrée*. (French was the language he preferred, and after the accident the only one he would speak.) On page 14, he refers to the United Nations, for whose library he did a mural, as the *Société des Nations*, the League of Nations.

27 These papers were actually rejects, as the bottom edges were so highly irregular that they were considered incomplete sheets, and the mill gave them to Tanya free of charge.

28 As recounted in Thomas Krens' *Helen Frankenthaler Prints: 1961-1979* (New York 1980), p 80.

29 For intaglio, a sheet of dampened paper is placed on a (usually copper) plate and passed through an etching press under tremendous pressure. The paper pulls the ink out of inked *depressions* made, by various means, in the plate. Lithography is *planographic* – the ink is on the surface.

30 This etching studio was located down a flight of stairs under the art studio built for Maurice; the two spaces comprised a new wing that had been added to the house.

31 While the artist and printer worked well together, there remained a personality conflict between Tanya and Steward that never improved (he finally left ULAE in 1974).

32 Tanya was a fourteen year old in Ekaterinburg in 1918 (where her father was publisher of *Ural Life*, the local newspaper) when the Tsar and his family were shot, in a house not too far away from her own.

1957–1982

ARTISTS & WRITERS

Rafael Alberti

Lee Bontecou

Jim Dine

Helen Frankenthaler

R. Buckminster Fuller

Fritz Glarner

Grace Hartigan

Jasper Johns

Kenneth Koch

Alexander Liberman

Marisol

Robert Motherwell

Barnett Newman

Frank O'Hara

Claes Oldenburg

Robert Rauschenberg

Larry Rivers

James Rosenquist

Edwin Schlossberg

Terry Southern

Saul Steinberg

Tony Towle

Cy Twombly

Andrei Voznesensky

PRINTERS

Frank Akers

Steven Anderson

Ben Berns

Robert Blackburn

Keith Brintzenhofe

Frank Burnham

Thomas Cox

Fred Genis

Bill Goldston

Maurice Grosman

Timothy Huchthausen

Glenn Lee

John Lund

Zigmunds Priede

Ester Pullman

Juda Rosenberg

James V. Smith

Danny Socha

Dick Sonnen

Donn Steward

Bill Taggart

David Umholtz

Jim Webb

Dan Welden

Craig Zammiello

LARRY RIVERS AND FRANK O'HARA

Stones: Five O'Clock, 1958

portfolio of lithographs, each sheet 19 X 23 1/4 IN.

PLATE 1

16/23

PLATE 2

JASPER JOHNS
Flag I, 1960
lithograph, 22 1/4 x 30 IN.
Tony and Gail Ganz

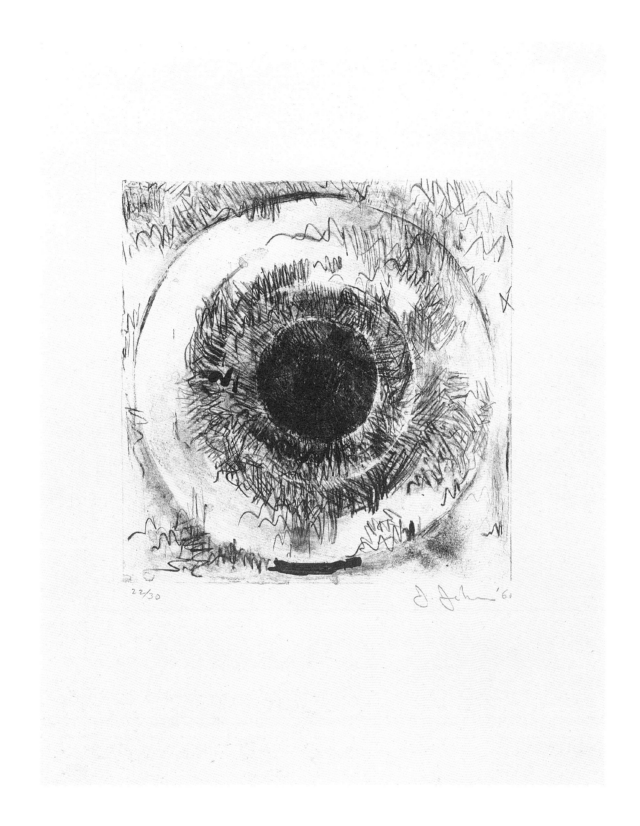

22/30   J. Johns '61

JASPER JOHNS   PLATE 3
Target, 1960
lithograph, 22 1/2 X 17 1/2 IN.
Jane Fearer Safer

PLATE 4

LARRY RIVERS
Jack of Spades, 1960
lithograph, 42 3/8 x 30 IN.

PLATE 5

HELEN FRANKENTHALER
First Stone, 1961
lithograph, 22 1/4 X 29 7/8 IN.
Mr. and Mrs. Sheldon Soffer, Teaneck, New Jersey

PLATE 6

JASPER JOHNS
False Start I, 1962
lithograph, 31 1/2 X 22 1/2 IN.
Private Collection

PLATE 7

ROBERT MOTHERWELL
Poet I, 1961–62
lithograph, 30 x 22 1/8 in.
Douglas and Leslie Volle

PLATE 8

ROBERT RAUSCHENBERG
License, 1962
lithograph, 41 1/4 x 29 1/2 IN.
Renie and Stan Helfgott

PLATE 9

LEE BONTECOU
Fourth Stone, 1963
lithograph, 41 1/2 x 29 5/8 IN.
Robert and Jane Meyerhoff, Phoenix, Maryland

artist Proof F.G.

PLATE 10

FRITZ GLARNER
Colored Drawing, 1963
lithograph, 24 3/4 x 20 IN.

B/c 5/10

63

PLATE 11

JASPER JOHNS,
0-9 B/C, page five, 1960–63
portfolio of lithographs, each sheet 20 1/2 x 15 1/2 IN.

PLATE 12

ROBERT RAUSCHENBERG
Accident, 1963
lithograph, 41 1/4 X 29 1/2 IN.
Lent by the artist

LARRY RIVERS
French Money, 1963
lithograph, 22 1/2 X 31 1/2 IN.
National Gallery of Art, Washington, Gift of the Woodward Foundation, Washington, D.C.

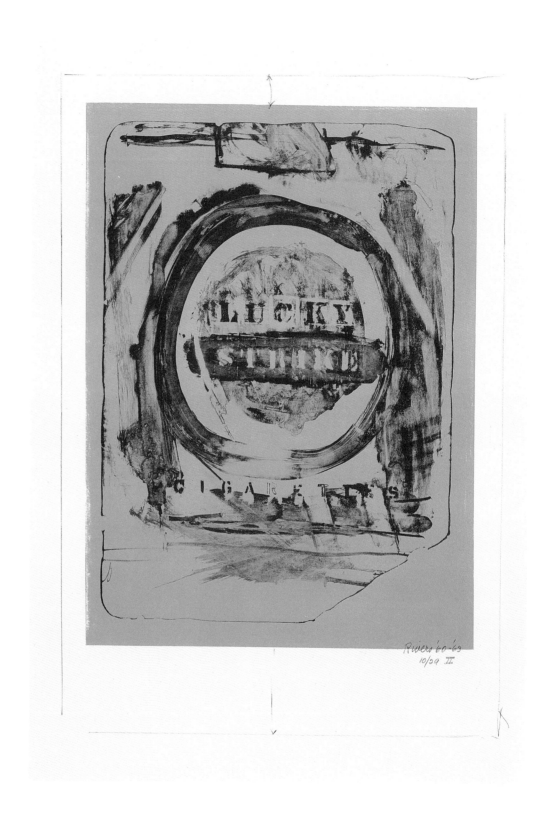

PLATE 14

LARRY RIVERS
Lucky Strike II, 1960–63
lithograph, 29 5/8 x 20 3/4 IN.

JASPER JOHNS

Ale Cans, 1964

lithograph, 22 1/2 x 17 1/2 IN.

Private Collection, courtesy of the Thomas Segal Gallery, Baltimore, Maryland

PLATE 15

PLATE 16

BARNETT NEWMAN
18 Cantos, title page, 1963–64
portfolio of lithographs, sheet size varies, this sheet 25 1/4 x 19 3/4 IN.
Robert and Jane Meyerhoff, Phoenix, Maryland

JIM DINE
Boot Silhouettes, 1965
lithograph, 41 1/2 X 29 7/8 IN.
Peter and Susan Ralston

PLATE 17

Double Apple Palette with Gingham 1965 Jim Dine 17/23

PLATE 18

JIM DINE
Double Apple Palette with Gingham, 1965
lithograph with gingham collage, 23 1/4 X 28 IN.
Peter and Susan Ralston

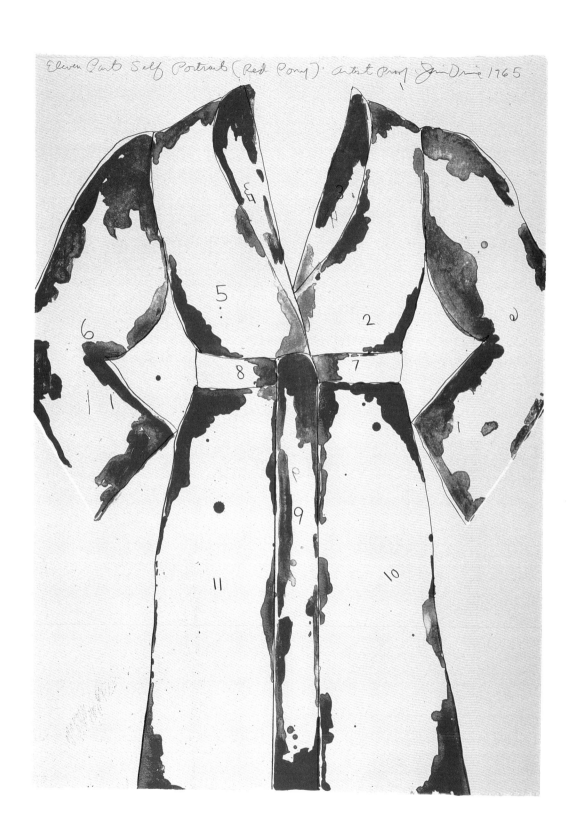

JIM DINE

Eleven Part Self Portrait (Red Pony), 1964-65

lithograph, 41 1/4 X 29 5/8 IN.

Carol and Morton Rapp

PLATE 19

PLATE 20

MARISOL
Pappagallo, 1965
lithograph, 25 5/8 x 19 in.

17/34 Rauschenberg 65

PLATE 21

ROBERT RAUSCHENBERG
Breakthrough II, 1965
lithograph, 48 3/8 x 34 IN.
Renie and Stan Helfgott

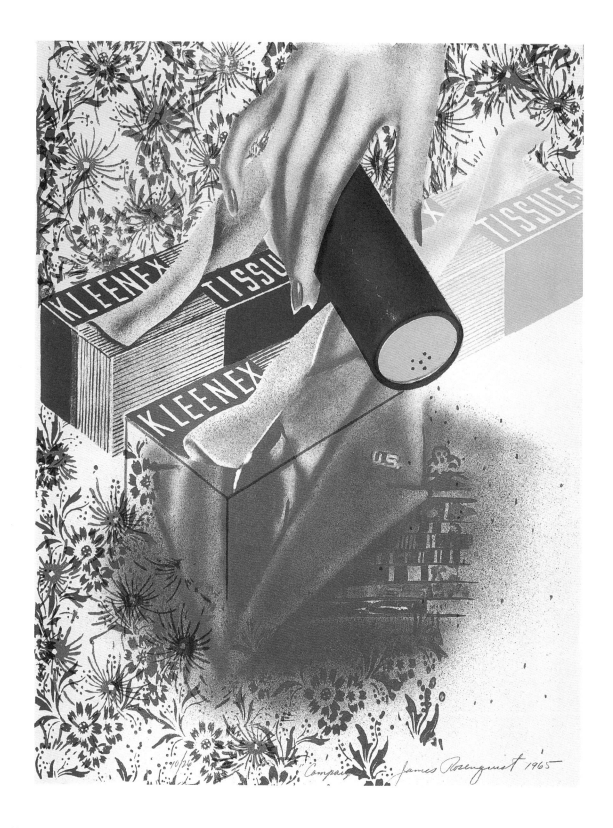

PLATE 22

JAMES ROSENQUIST
Campaign, 1965
lithograph, 29 3/8 x 22 3/8 IN.

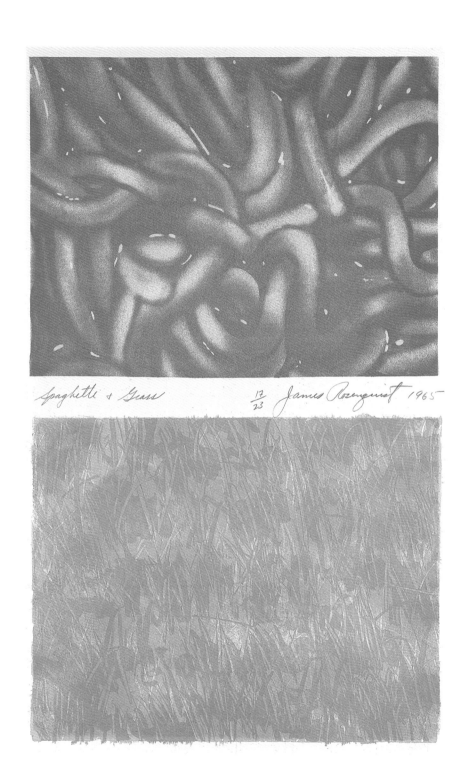

Spaghetti & Grass 17/23 James Rosenquist 1965

PLATE 23

JAMES ROSENQUIST
Spaghetti and Grass, 1964–65
lithograph, 31 1/4 x 22 1/4 IN.
Fearer Family Collection

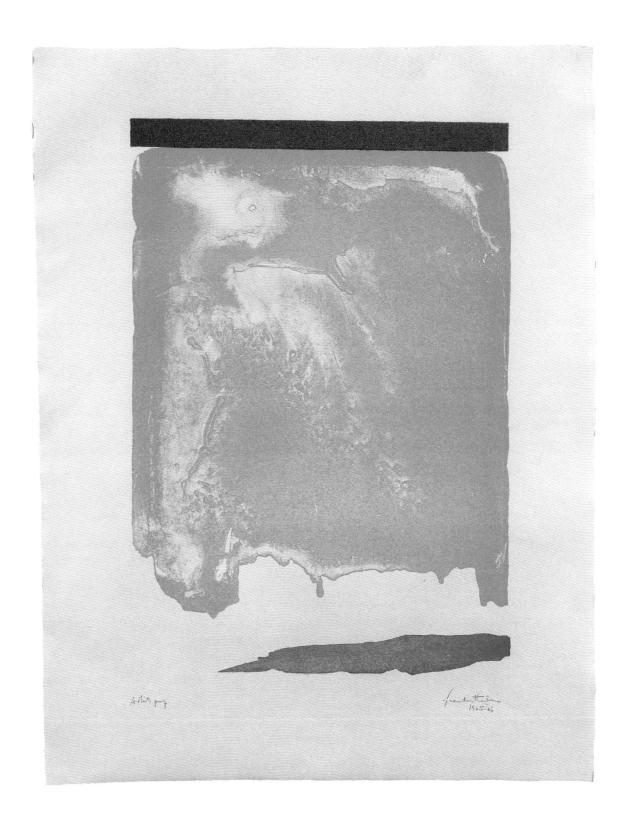

PLATE 24

HELEN FRANKENTHALER
Persian Garden, 1965–66
lithograph, 25 3/4 x 20 in.
Lent by the artist

"Atalanta In Arcadia" A.P. Hartigan 1962-66

PLATE 25

GRACE HARTIGAN
The Archaics: Atalanta in Arcadia, 1962–66
lithograph, 27 1/2 x 19 7/8 IN.

"From Eyes Blue and Cold"

Artist's Proof
Hartigan 1962-66

PLATE 26

GRACE HARTIGAN
The Archaics: From Eyes Blue and Cold, 1962–66
lithograph, 27 1/2 x 19 7/8 in.

"In the Campagna" A.P. Hartigan 1962-66

PLATE 27

GRACE HARTIGAN
The Archaics: In the Campagna, 1962–66
lithograph, 27 1/2 x 19 7/8 IN.

Circles of Confusion   Artist's Proof ⅛   Jim Rosenquist 1966

PLATE 28

JAMES ROSENQUIST
Circles of Confusion I, 1965–66
lithograph, 38 3/8 x 28 IN.
Personal Collection of Leo Castelli, New York

PLATE 29

JAMES ROSENQUIST
Expo 67 Mural - Firepole 33' x 17', 1967
lithograph, 34 X 18 7/8 IN.

PLATE 30

CY TWOMBLY
Note I, 1967
cancellation proof
intaglio, 25 7/8 x 20 3/8 IN.

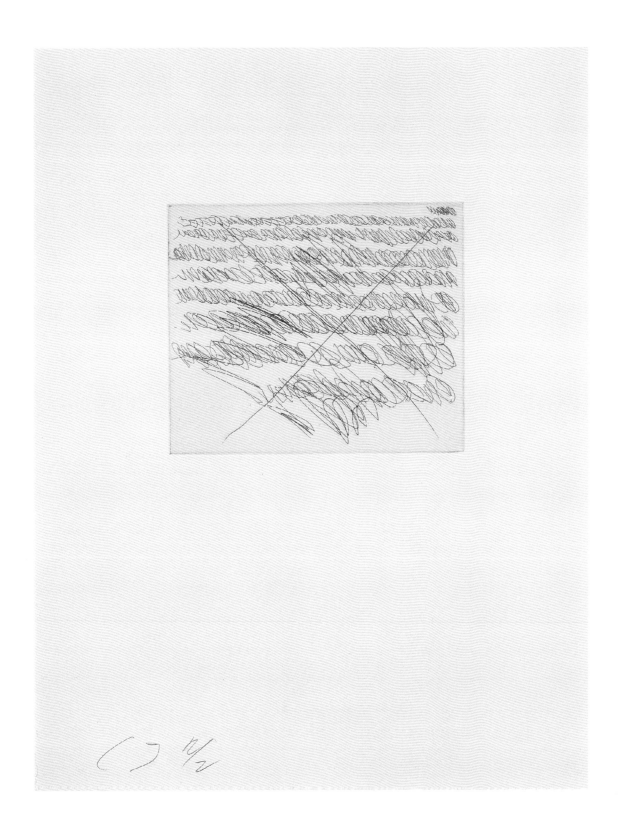

PLATE 31

CY TWOMBLY
Note II, 1967
cancellation proof
intaglio, 25 1/2 X 20 1/4 IN.

PLATE 32

CY TWOMBLY
Note III, 1967
cancellation proof
intaglio, 25 5/8 x 20 3/8 IN.

CY TWOMBLY

Note IV, 1967
cancellation proof
intaglio, 25 3/8 x 20 1/4 IN.

PLATE 33

PLATE 34

LEE BONTECOU AND TONY TOWLE
Fifth Stone, Sixth Stone, 1967–68
unbound book of intaglios, each sheet 20 x 26 1/4 IN.

PLATE 35

LEE BONTECOU
Seventh Stone, 1965–68
lithograph, 24 7/8 x 19 7/8 IN.

PLATE 36

FRITZ GLARNER
Recollection, cover, 1964–68
portfolio of lithographs, each sheet 14 3/4 x 23 IN.

PLATE 37

Note X - State I 1968
7/7

BARNETT NEWMAN
Notes: Note X - State I, 1968
portfolio of intaglios, each sheet 19 7/8 x 14 IN.
Jasper Johns

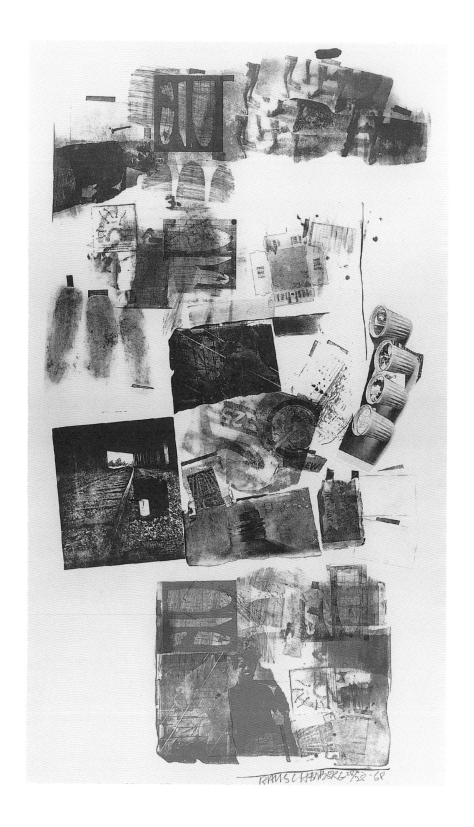

ROBERT RAUSCHENBERG
Water Stop, 1968
lithograph and intaglio, 54 1/8 x 31 5/8 IN.
The Schweber Family

PLATE 39

EDWIN SCHLOSSBERG
WORDSWORDSWORDS, 1967–68
unbound book of lithographs, intaglios, and embossing, each sheet 11 x 8 1/2 IN.
Robert and Brenda Edelson, Baltimore, Maryland

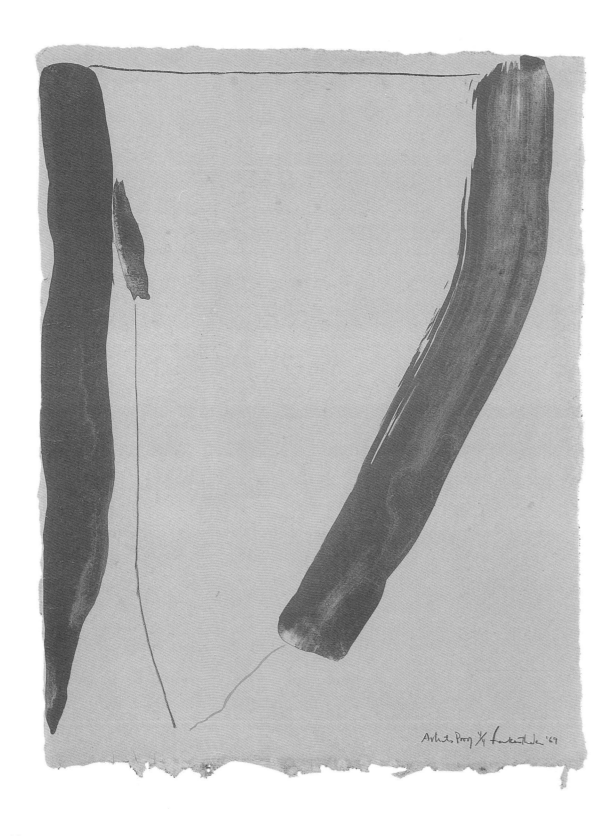

PLATE 40

HELEN FRANKENTHALER
A Slice of the Stone Itself, 1969
lithograph, 19 x 15 IN.
Lent anonymously

PLATE 41

HELEN FRANKENTHALER
Lot's Wife, 1970-71
triptych lithograph, 137 5/8 x 36 3/4 IN.

PLATE 42

JASPER JOHNS
Decoy, 1971
lithograph, 41 x 29 IN.
Brian Goldston

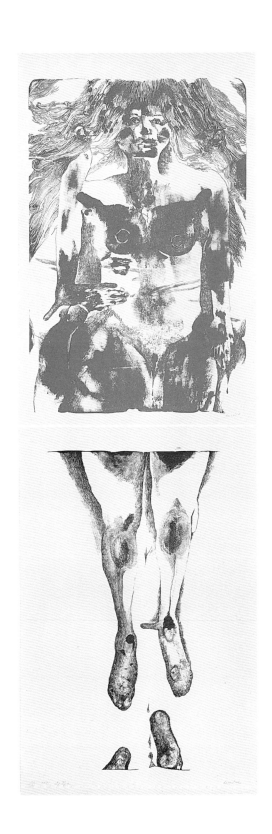

MARISOL

Diptych, 1971

lithograph, 95 1/2 x 31 5/8 in.

PLATE 43

PLATE 44

ROBERT MOTHERWELL
Samurai, 1971
lithograph, 72 5/8 x 36 7/8 IN.

PLATE 45

LARRY RIVERS
For Adults Only, 1971
lithograph, 70 1/2 x 29 1/2 IN.

PLATE 46

LEE BONTECOU
Fourteenth Stone, 1968–72
lithograph, 28 x 39 3/4 IN.

JIM DINE
2 Hearts (The Donut), 1970–72
diptych lithograph, 54 x 63 1/2 in.
Nancy and Tom Driscoll

PLATE 47

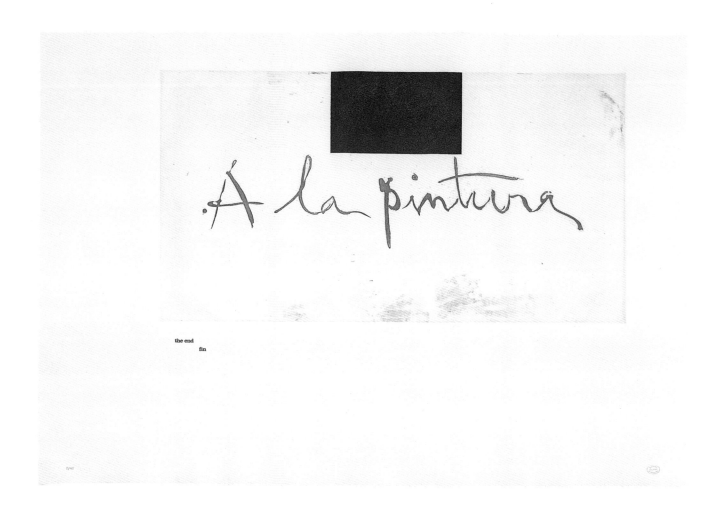

the end
fin

PLATE 48

ROBERT MOTHERWELL AND RAFAEL ALBERTI
A la pintura, end page, 1968–72
unbound book of intaglios, each sheet 25 3/4 x 38 1/8 in.
Renie and Stan Helfgott

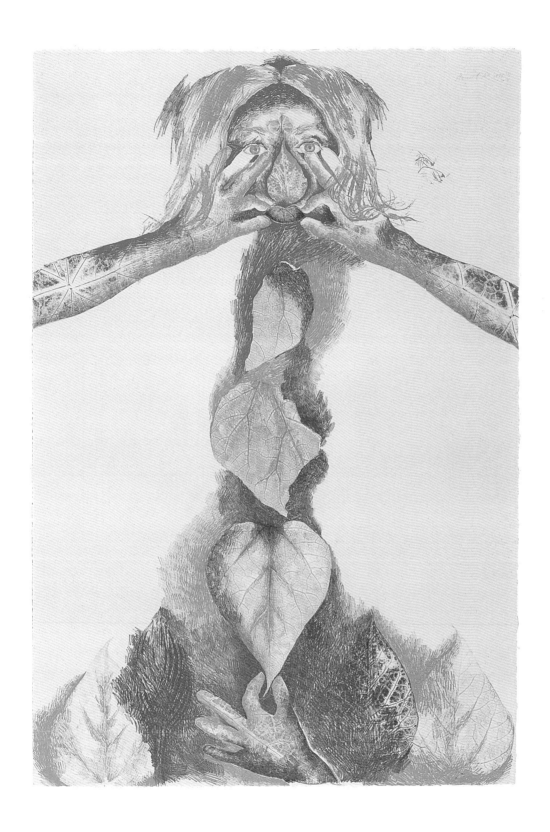

MARISOL

Catalpa Maiden About to Touch Herself, 1973
lithograph, 40 1/4 x 27 3/4 IN.

PLATE 49

PLATE 50

SAUL STEINBERG
The Museum, 1972
lithograph, 20 3/4 x 28 1/8 in.

SAUL STEINBERG

Main Street, 1972–73
lithograph, 22 5/8 x 30 IN.
John and Christina Lund

PLATE 51

PLATE 52

HELEN FRANKENTHALER
East and Beyond, 1972-73
woodcut, 31 7/8 X 22 IN.
Carol and Morton Rapp

AP 3/4

Frankenthaler '74

HELEN FRANKENTHALER   PLATE 53
Savage Breeze, 1974
woodcut, 31 1/2 x 27 1/4 IN.

PLATE 54

ROBERT RAUSCHENBERG
Kitty Hawk, 1974
lithograph, 78 5/8 x 40 1/8 IN.

PLATE 55

ROBERT RAUSCHENBERG
Tanya, 1974
lithograph with embossing, 22 1/2 x 15 3/8 IN.

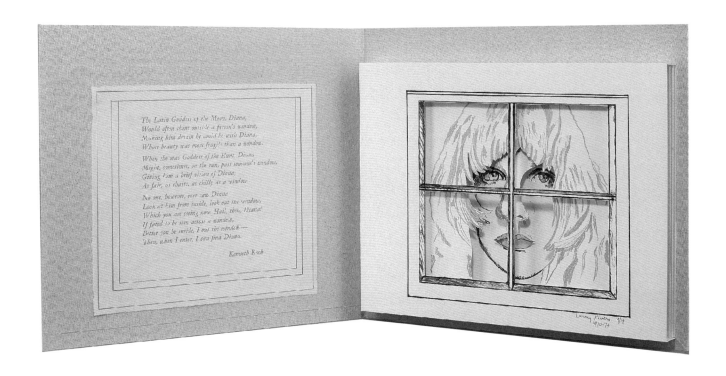

The Latin Goddess of the Moon, Diana,
Would often stare outside a person's window,
Making him dream he could be with Diana,
Whose beauty was more fragile than a window.

When she was Goddess of the Hunt, Diana
Might, sometimes, on the run, pass someone's window,
Giving him a brief vision of Diana,
As fair, as chaste, as chilly as a window.

No one, however, ever saw Diana
Look at him from inside, look out the window,
Which you are seeing now. Hail, thou, Diana!
If fated to be seen across a window,
Better you be inside, I out the window —
Then, when I enter, I can find Diana.

                        Kenneth Koch

PLATE 56

LARRY RIVERS AND KENNETH KOCH
Diana with Poem, 1970-74
three-dimensional lithograph, 22 5/8 x 26 5/8 IN.

PLATE 57

JAMES ROSENQUIST
Off the Continental Divide, 1973-74
lithograph, 43 X 79 1/8 IN.

PLATE 58

CY TWOMBLY
Untitled I, 1967, published 1974
intaglio, 27 1/2 X 40 5/8 IN.

PLATE 59

CY TWOMBLY
Untitled II, 1967, published 1974
intaglio, 27 3/8 x 40 3/8 IN.
Peter and Susan Ralston

PLATE 60

CY TWOMBLY
Sketches, 1967–75
portfolio of intaglios, each sheet 8 1/2 X 12 1/4 IN.
Robert Rauschenberg

CLAES OLDENBURG

Tea Pot, 1975

lithograph, 18 1/4 x 26 1/4 IN.

PLATE 61

PLATE 62

JASPER JOHNS
Scent, 1975-76
lithograph, linocut and woodcut, 31 1/4 x 47 IN.
Renie and Stan Helfgott

R. Buckminster Fuller

Tetrascroll, 1975–77

book of lithographs bound with Dacron polyester sailcloth, each sheet 35 1/2 x 35 1/2 x 35 1/2 IN.

PLATE 63

PLATE 64

LARRY RIVERS AND TERRY SOUTHERN
The Donkey and the Darling, 1967–77
unbound book of lithographs, each sheet 18 1/2 x 24 1/2 IN.

ALEXANDER LIBERMAN AND ANDREI VOZNESENSKY

Nostalgia for the Present, 1977-79
unbound book of lithographs, each sheet 40 3/4 x 27 1/4 IN.

PLATE 65

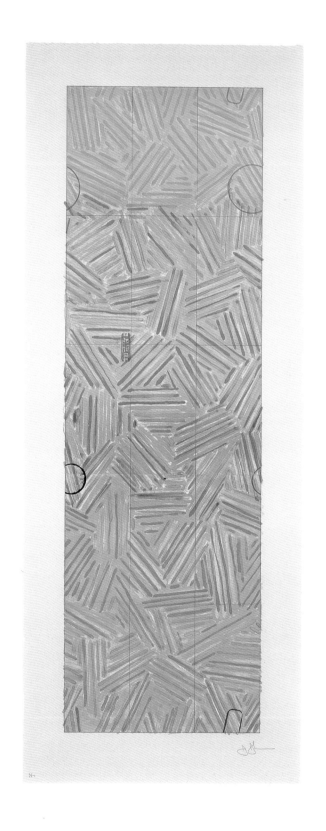

PLATE 66

PLATE 67

JAMES ROSENQUIST
Chambers, 1980
lithograph, 30 X 47 1/8 IN.
Mr. and Mrs. Dennis Kannenberg

PLATE 68

EDWIN SCHLOSSBERG
Edges Strengthen, 1981
lithograph, 41 7/8 x 29 5/8 IN.

EDWIN SCHLOSSBERG
Warm Memories, 1981
lithograph, 19 1/8 x 25 3/4 IN.

PLATE 69

PLATE 70

LEE BONTECOU
An Untitled Print, 1981–82
lithograph, 93 x 42 IN.

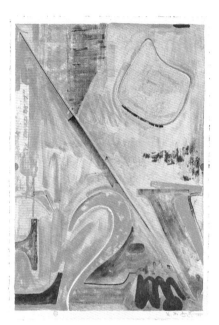

PLATE 71

JASPER JOHNS
Voice 2, 1982
three-panel lithograph, each sheet 35 3/4 x 24 1/4 IN.
Lent anonymously

PLATE 72

JAMES ROSENQUIST
Dog Descending a Staircase, 1980–82
lithograph and intaglio, 42 X 70 IN.

BILL GOLDSTON

Since the death of Tatyana Grosman in 1982, the legendary workshop has continued to be a unique center for the production of artists' prints. The successes of the past fifteen years are owed largely to the guidance of Bill Goldston, who arrived at ULAE in 1969. Goldston has always adhered to Grosman's near-mystical belief in the sacred nature of the artist's mark, her refusal to compromise, her persistence in courting artists, and her willingness to wait years for an artist to complete an edition.

Goldston's first introduction to the studio came through his professor of lithography at the University of Minnesota, Zigmunds Priede, who had been a printer at ULAE during the summers. Impressed by Goldston's enthusiasm for lithography and creativity in exploring techniques, Priede invited Goldston, then a MFA student, to print at ULAE in the summer of 1967. However, Goldston was drafted into the Army, and was unable to begin working until July 1969.

Upon arriving, Goldston immediately set to work on a project of Robert Rauschenberg's involving photosensitive stones, an idea that Priede had conceived to make the surface of a stone sensitive to light, then project photo images onto the stone, and print the images as lithographs on paper. However, the studio was busy that summer and before Rauschenberg arrived Goldston proofed prints for Helen Frankenthaler, Jasper Johns, Jim Dine, and James Rosenquist until his return to Minnesota in September.

ROBERT RAUSCHENBERG WORKING ON PHOTOSENSITIVE STONES. ULAE STUDIO. AUGUST 1969.

BILL GOLDSTON, ANDREI VOZNESENSKY, ROBERT RAUSCHENBERG, AND TATYANA GROSMAN. ULAE STUDIO. 1977

Goldston returned to ULAE the following summer to help in the studio. Though Grosman was a notorious perfectionist and often difficult to please, Goldston notes that "Once you worked with Tanya and you established a relationship with her, it was almost impossible to free yourself from that because of your own interest in her as a human being. Her devotion to what she was doing made you want to help her." By the end of January 1971, Goldston moved his family to Long Island and, along with the intaglio printer Donn Steward, began working full time for ULAE. Goldston quickly moved into a leadership position and upon the death of her husband in 1976, Grosman encouraged Goldston to take charge of running both the studio and the business. At times he compares the running of the studio to that of the evolution of a painting, "It goes in a direction and you simply follow it and tomorrow is a different day."

By the 1980s Goldston was familiar with all aspects of the business and was ready to return to the initial spirit of the studio. He purchased different and larger presses and established two additional off-site workshops, one primarily for intaglio near the house on Skidmore Place and the other in the TriBeCa section of Manhattan. The latter gave the artists with young children the flexibility to work unusual hours and remain close to home. By 1995, their children were old enough to be left at school for the day and the artists chose to return to the studios on Long Island. The TriBeCa studio was closed, and a 7,000 square foot, multipurpose studio was opened less than three miles from Skidmore

Place. Today, everything from lithography, intaglio, and silkscreen, to the building of crates, goes on at the building the employees call "Clinton."

In guiding ULAE's expansion, Goldston has maintained the sense of community and spirit always associated with the house on Skidmore Place. Only one artist is scheduled to visit the studio on a given day. That artist and between five to seven printers, additional ULAE staff, interns, and visiting collectors, writers, or curators, are served a traditional family-style lunch. Business is still conducted at one end of the house while prints are stored and shown upstairs in a small attic room. The center of the house holds rows of worn lithographic stones and a handfed transfer press that Grosman had installed in the late 1950s. All of this is essential to the business' success and all of it is part of history. The deep appreciation for the struggles of one woman to establish the press and its almost magical prosperity over forty years is why artists continue to make the trip out to Long Island.

THE ARTISTS

While the publishing of an artist's print is possible only through symbiosis, the artist's act of creation is at the heart of the process. Grosman had the ability to select artists that not only interested her, but who are now among the most influential masters of the late twentieth century: Jim Dine, Helen Frankenthaler, Jasper Johns, Robert Motherwell, Barnett Newman, Robert Rauschenberg, and James Rosenquist.

No new artists had joined the ULAE "family" since the early seventies and by 1982 Goldston knew it was time for the studio to move in a younger direction. "That was the spirit engendered by Tanya from the begin-

ROBERT RAUSCHENBERG (LEFT) AND BILL GOLDSTON (RIGHT), ULAE STUDIO, 1978.

ning. When Jasper first came, he was not a well-known artist. He was thirty years old. There were older, established artists, such as Motherwell, Glarner, and Newman. But Tanya's emphasis was with artists like Larry Rivers, Robert Rauschenberg, Jim Dine, Marisol, and James Rosenquist. I was just following Tanya's lead."

At this writing, two of the twelve artists currently working at ULAE – Rauschenberg and Johns – have been with the workshop since its inception. Each of the artists selected by Goldston to carry on the tradition has an individual aesthetic that is appropriate to the workshop, but also reflects a personal sensibility. Five are women.

The wave of artists who began printing at ULAE in the early eighties includes Terry Winters, Bill Jensen, Susan Rothenberg, Carroll Dunham, and Elizabeth Murray. If they do not reflect everything that was happening in the art world at the time – missing are artists who were identified with neo-geo, conceptual art, and the machismo neo-expressionist movement – they indicate a move away from a pop sensibility, for which ULAE was known in the early years, toward the more painterly. Each of the five plays lovingly with forms, images, and textures. Concepts are means to explore formal concerns. Stylistically diverse, Rothenberg and Murray both use imagery – horses and people (Rothenberg) and cups, chairs, and musical instruments (Murray) – as departure points for their particular brand of abstraction. Winters' and Dunham's imagery is oblique, drawn from musings on physics, botany, and medicine. Jensen's pure abstractions correlate to the mystical shapes of Goya and the work of the early modernists.

The four artists who came to ULAE in the nineties are Jane Hammond, Kiki Smith, Julian Lethbridge, and Suzanne McClelland. The work of each is strikingly different from that of the others, mirroring the pluralism of the art world. McClelland and Lethbridge both begin with abstraction but McClelland explores gestural abstraction and word imagery while Lethbridge encompasses a more formal and cerebral enterprise. Hammond has developed a personal lexicon of found imagery – 276 images culled from numerous sources, ages, cultures – to convey both a personal and universal view of the world. In many ways, her work is a return to the pop sensibility of the early years. Kiki Smith, a sculptor who works with the terrain of the body, is the leader of an unofficial movement that arose in the mid-eighties. She is heir apparent to Rauschenberg, both for her extensive use of photography in printmaking and her mastery of collage.

TERRY WINTERS

In November 1982, while traveling the country showing prints, Goldston became aware of Terry Winters' work at the Delahunty Gallery in Dallas, and there arranged a studio visit. Ironically, the two met by chance a few nights later at the opening of an exhibition of paintings by Bill Jensen.

For years Winters had been following the work of Johns and Rauschenberg at ULAE, contemplating the idea of making prints there. When asked by Goldston, he enthusiastically accepted the invitation and in late 1982 made the trip to West Islip. He was the first artist who came to maturity in the eighties to print at ULAE.

Winters immediately began working in lithography. His first print *Ova*, 1982, took him only a month

to complete and was as much about exploring a new medium as it was about creating a final product. He found himself seduced by the technique, the similarities to drawing, and the involvement of the printers in his imagery. Following *Ova* was *Factors of Increase*, 1983, a lithograph from two stones and two plates in which Winters began to explore the organic imagery of his paintings and drawings. He describes this print as "my tentative way into finding a place for lithography in the body of work I was trying to build." The print evolved out of techniques and processes unique to lithography.

Winters' subsequent endeavors became progressively complex as he grew more comfortable with technique. At the same time, accustomed to the feel of paper and large oil sticks that left heavy, textured marks, he felt frustrated by an inability to achieve the thick layering and play of light characteristic of his drawings. As a solution, Goldston suggested that Winters draw directly on paper and then transfer the drawing to a lithographic plate using solvents, a technique developed to transfer newspaper images in early Rauschenberg prints.

Winters' first series of prints to use this transfer process was *Morula I, II,* and *III,* 1983-84, and *Double Standard*, 1984. *Morula I* incorporated one stone and three plates; *Morula II*, three stones and five plates; *Morula III*, eight plates; and *Double Standard*, eighteen plates. Each uses the same image of clustered cells. Each is a step in the artist's process of "looking" at the same image in different ways. This series with its mixture of the micro/macroscopic view of the world, parallels changes taking place in the imagery of Winters' painting and marks his ability to work on a print with freedom, without worrying about how it is going to translate when it is drawn on the plate.

Folio, 1986, a portfolio of eleven lithographs including a title page and colophon, demonstrates Winters' sense that lithography is a medium between drawing and painting. Through the introduction of color, the use of the press as "a marking device," and the layering of plates, Winters discovered that he could build structure and create surface density, thus emulating aspects of his paintings. The entire printing of *Folio* was accomplished on the offset press, with Winters responding as the plates were printed and even drawing on the plate on the bed of the press.

By 1988, Winters was ready to try intaglio. His first print was *Station*, 1988, made from one copper plate. It was followed one year later by *Fourteen Etchings*, a portfolio in which he combines nineteenth-century x-rays with drawings and *Novalis*, an image that started on a lithographic plate in 1983. But the early nineties saw a change in Winters' structure and palette as his paintings moved away from earth tones to an explosion of color, and from biomorphic imagery to prismatic landscapes. Images such as *Theorem*, 1992, and *Locus*, 1993, come out of his struggle in dealing with the incorporation of color into his work, while *Models for Synthetic Pictures*, 1994, a portfolio of twelve intaglios, reveals the relationship between Winters' prints, drawings, and paintings. It also demonstrates his mastery of the technique by using only five plates and three colors – red, yellow, and blue – on each image.

BILL JENSEN

Bill Jensen was the first artist contacted by Goldston after the death of Grosman. Jensen and Goldston had

DOUGLAS VOLLE (LEFT) AND TERRY WINTERS (RIGHT), ULAE STUDIO, 1990.

been graduate students together at the University of Minnesota but had not spoken in almost ten years. At the time, Jensen was preparing for an exhibition of paintings in November 1982 and was unable to commit to work. Insistent that Jensen at least contemplate the idea, Goldston delivered some copper plates to his studio and agreed to contact him again in the future.

In 1983, Jensen lost his studio and after pressure from Goldston, agreed to use ULAE as a place for drawing until he could relocate. In February of that year, Jensen arrived at ULAE, and confronting the etching press immediately broke out in a cold sweat as he remembered a German etching professor at the University of Minnesota. The professor's methods had been so dictatorial that he had painted yellow footprints on the floor to indicate the exact steps to be taken when walking from the paper bath to the press to the drying rack. Jensen quit the class after two days. Fortunately, John Lund, a fellow student at the University, who joined ULAE in 1971 as a printer, sensed his anxiety and advised Jensen that, "there are no yellow footprints here. Copper is malleable, it is erasable. You can do whatever you want." This was enough for Jensen to set about working on a number of small etchings – the size of the notebook drawings he had brought with him. In retrospect, these first etchings, which Jensen refers to as his "baby steps," allowed him to learn the various intaglio processes – etching, open-bite, aquatint, engraving, roulette, and sugar-lift. Later, the eleven etchings were compiled in a portfolio entitled *Endless*, 1983–85, and exhibited at the Museum of Modern Art.

Endless was not only a doorway to technique; it also informed his paintings and drawings, which he scrapes and incises. The small scale of *Endless* and subsequent prints became, like his paintings and works on paper, a sharp contrast to the large canvases of other contemporary abstract painters. By the early eighties, Jensen had already attracted critical attention for his heavily impastoed surfaces, with their abstract explorations of shapes, that brought to mind the moody romanticism of Albert Pinkham Ryder and the clean landscapes of Marsden Hartley. Printmaking afforded him an opportunity to mine the emotional and psychological content of these shapes through a different medium.

Yet intaglio remains for Jensen a means to an end. As he once noted, "technique is only the tool to express the emotional content. And I think the more effortless you are with technique, the more the content can come through." Lund has remarked, "Bill is a tool user. There is a passion there, wanting to know how to do things, finding out what is possible on the plate, utilizing some other variety of technique with every print." Copper has a memory for markmaking and Jensen takes advantage of this unique attribute, considering the process more important than the end product.

Vanquished, 1988–89, was the biggest plate Jensen had worked on, approaching the scale of his paintings. He also began to emulate more closely his process of painting – putting something down and then taking it off. In etching, this was accomplished by laying down aquatints that he could then go back and scrape and burnish. The result was that the layers of color sat on each other, emulating the texture of his paintings. More recently, he and printer Jihong Shi have taken intaglio one step closer to painting by figuring a way to use various substances, such as automotive two-

BILL JENSEN, ULAE STUDIO, 1996.

part epoxy, or bonding, and polyurethane to build upon the copper plate as opposed to scraping into the plate, creating various layers and textures in and on the plate.

If Jensen's painting influenced his printmaking, the opposite is also true. The organic process – working simultaneously on an etching, painting, and gouache, and making changes on the plate that will then affect the painting or vice-versa – has resulted in a number of related paintings, drawings, and intaglios. A remarkable example is his most recent print *Defiance*, 1996, where a richness and depth of color both relate to and expand upon the painting of the same title.

Susan Rothenberg

Goldston came across Susan Rothenberg's painting *Creek* at the 1983 Whitney *Biennial* and thought it was one of the most beautiful paintings he had ever seen. "It was something that moved me emotionally," says Goldston, "and I thought I would have to be crazy not to work with someone who could make a painting like that." When Goldston contacted Rothenberg the rapport was immediate and soon after she began working at ULAE.

Rothenberg started with lithography, and although she had used the process before with Maurice Sanchez at Derrière L'Etoile Studios, she considered herself a novice in the medium. She points out, however, that her continued excitement with the medium came from the fact that the printers at ULAE "welcomed ignorance in the name of invention." From her previous experiences, Rothenberg understood that she needed to simplify her approach to counter her inclination to overwork the stone or plate, but, in the process, she did not want to sacrifice the surface, texture, and means of burying the image that were so essential to her paintings. In response, Goldston developed a greasier, darker lithography crayon – made by soaking charcoal in oil – which Rothenberg used for *Plug*, 1983, her first lithograph at ULAE, and many editions to follow.

Rothenberg's next two prints, *Four Green Lines*, 1984, and *Between the Eyes*, 1983-84, were breakthroughs for the artist as she discovered how to erase. Although these prints are lithographs, using this technique allowed her to work from dark to light, finding her images and figures within an established ground, as she does with her paintings and drawings. *Between the Eyes* was also her first print to incorporate woodcut. The block was printed twice in the same place, achieving the layering she was accustomed to in her paintings. The imagery derives from her interest in Piet Mondrian, relating to a passage she read about him coming to New York. Rothenberg portrays him standing before the New York skyline with the Brooklyn Bridge in the distance. The collaged yellow paper and red fingermark are tributes to the artist. His influence on her work can also be seen in the woodcut, *Blue Violin*, 1986, where the background is divided into four squares, colored red, blue, yellow, and gray.

Rothenberg continued with her experimentation, pushing herself to new levels of discovery, with *Missing Corners*, 1984, a series of eighteen monoprints on a Mexican handmade paper. The print resulted from a piece of wood she found, carved, and brought to ULAE. She asked printer Keith Brintzenhofe to proof the image in both red and black, but unsatisfied with the way the image looked, she began to mix the two inks directly on the block with her fingers. As there was no way to replicate the color achieved by Rothenberg's handwork in the ordinary printmaking process, she continued to color the block each time the sheet was run through the press, making every print unique. This new technique combined with erasure led to prints such as *Black Water*, 1985-86, and *Stumblebum*, 1986. Both images began with Rothenberg applying ink onto stones with her fingers, and removing it as she saw fit to enhance the image.

After her extensive work in lithography, it was an obvious progression for Rothenberg to move into mezzotint, an intaglio process that offers the possibility of working from dark to light. Rothenberg welcomed the physical aspects of mezzotint that seemed to burden other artists. The worked copper plate also provided a rich, textural background similar to the ground she laid for her paintings. Rothenberg dedicated three years at ULAE to mezzotint, accomplishing four editions: *Yellow Spinner*, 1988; *Three Parts*, 1987-88; *Mezzo Fist #1*, 1990; and *Mezzo Fist #2*, 1990.

Carroll Dunham

Goldston met Carroll Dunham through Winters in 1984 while Dunham was working part time as a designer at a magazine. Impressed with his potential, Goldston suggested that he give up his job and dedicate all of his time to being an artist. "If you are living off your own gifts, your own means, your own wits, it's different. What I wanted Tip to feel was, that it's high risk, you don't know where your next meal is coming from. That is important because that energy then goes into the work. It gives it the edge." With that commitment from Dunham, Goldston brought a stone and some litho crayons to his studio.

Dunham had no printmaking experience beyond undergraduate coursework in etching and silkscreen, and, accustomed to painting and drawing, was disoriented by the stone. He found himself focused on the idea that he wasn't working on the actual artwork, that the act of drawing on the stone was an incremental step to the final outcome. What Dunham did not understand about this "interim step" – but quickly learned after several disappointing proofs – was its complexity, which involved building an image not only by drawing but through layering stones and/or plates. Like Winters, Dunham's evolution from his early, tentative lithographs (both *Untitled* prints from 1984-85, from two stones) to a more complex procedure, happened very quickly. After experimenting with and then rejecting ways of introducing the wood-grain imagery of his paintings into his lithographs, he began working on the print *Accelerator*, 1985, using imagery that resembled hundreds of exploding balls. The idea for the print was conceived while he was reading about particle accelerators, interesting him in depicting objects both frontally and spinning in space. However, when he drew the balls on the stone, he found the image to be too flat. To counter the problem, printer Brintzenhofe proposed that Dunham draw the balls on mylar, masking them on the various layers so that they would appear to be overlapping or nested together, consequently creating an illusion of depth. The mylar images were then photo-transferred to four stones and two plates and printed on both the transfer and offset presses.

Color Message A, B, and *C*, 1985-86, are Dunham's first prints to incorporate color and served as a prelude to the larger, more complex *Full Spectrum*, 1985-87. In this print, Dunham was simultaneously exploring the added complexity of color, the four-color printing process, and the regeneration of the flying ring from his paintings. As advanced technically as *Accelerator* is, *Full Spectrum* is also beautifully pure in its approach, involving a single stone or plate for each of the colors of the rainbow.

CARROLL DUNHAM, ULAE STUDIO, 1989.

For Dunham, his next set of prints, *Red Shift*, 1987-88, was a "punctuation mark" in both his printmaking and painting careers. He was ready to move away from wood as a material and as a subject in his paintings, and seeing his images come together on clean, white sheets of paper gave him the confidence to begin constructing new subjects within his paintings. The prints and the process of making them caused Dunham to realize that there were other ways to do things. "I knew from working on the lithos that there was a very different way that my work could look and I could still feel connected to it as my work. I didn't just have to work one way." The portfolio, made from eighteen stones and twenty-two aluminum plates, took two years to complete and reflects his ease with the technique. The loose and open way of working, where one plate has a smear of tusche and another has a line drawing, enabled him to create the illusion of depth much sought after in his earlier prints.

Dunham moved for a time from lithography to intaglio. He began his intaglios tentatively, first making full, rich, little prints using the same imagery as in his paintings. He remembers being amazed at the amount of information that a copper plate could hold. "Like a computer chip, its capacity seemed infinite," he says. Then Goldston showed Dunham some plates made from pewter. Dunham took an immediate liking to this material because drawing on it, he recalls, "was like drawing on butter." Pewter has a softness to it that gives prints a certain romantic quality but it also degenerates quickly and, as a result, produces small editions. Therefore, *Shadows*, 1989, Dunham's portfolio of ten drypoints from ten pewter plates, is only an edition of fourteen.

Out of these early experiences came a number of lithographs and intaglios, but most notably, a series of large-scale intaglios that includes *Untitled*, 1988-89; *Wave*, 1988-90; *Point of Origin*, 1988-92; and *Another Dimension*, 1988-95. All four of the prints use the same imagery as in Dunham's paintings – columns, t-shaped waves, and mounds of color, references to mountains rising out of or sinking into the landscape – and were achieved through diverse, chemistry classlike experiments, using water, oil, alcohol, acid, and an array of different powders.

ELIZABETH MURRAY

Elizabeth Murray came to ULAE in 1986. A distinguished draftsman, Murray began working in lithography. Her first lithograph, *#1*, 1986, comprising thirteen stones, explores the domestic and musical imagery of her paintings from the same time: an upside-down table, vases, and a guitar played by a disembodied hand. Lines are gestural, while colors are layered and translucent. In *Blue Body*, 1986-87, Murray confronts the complexities of the medium. She expands the scale of the table and guitar, which consume much of the sheet, and works on both plates and stones, building up the density of color and illusion of texture.

When considered in sequence, Murray's prints reveal her desire to surpass previous accomplishments, to bring something new to the process while integrating it with her painting and drawing. She describes printmaking as "about discovery...the printers are tuned into that and dedicated to it. At ULAE you never hear, oh we can't do that." For her next two prints, *Up Dog*, 1987-88, and *Down Dog*, 1988, Goldston and printer Brintzenhofe devised a way to print from several matrices, hand-tearing, and reassembling the prints

ELIZABETH MURRAY
WORKING ON *UP DOG* AND
DOWN DOG ULAE STUDIO,
1988.

using tabs. The forms are broken and relate to her paintings, the cartoonlike imagery has now been extended to the edges of the paper and depth is achieved through the building of layers and colors.

After the completion of *Down Dog*, Murray began a series of intaglio projects which went on simultaneously at both the Long Island and TriBeCa studios. The first four prints completed were part of a series titled *Quartet*, 1988-89, and although they are small in size – the image measures 8 x 6 inches – these prints capture the explosiveness and fragmentation of her paintings. *Her Story*, a collaborative book with the poet Anne Waldman, was a continuation of Murray's fascination with intaglio and an extension of her experience with lithography. To make the book, a series of Murray's drawings were transferred to lithographic plates and printed on the handfed offset press. At the same time Murray etched similar drawings onto copper plates of the same size. These were printed on top of the lithographs and then pasted down on handmade paper watermarked with her signature and Waldman's. In *Undoing*, 1989-90, Murray continues the explorations begun in *Down Dog*, while building on her experience with the intaglio process. Through a combination of etching, aquatint, drypoint, and lithography on three sheets of overlaid paper, *Undoing* combines Murray's characteristic gestural lines with delicate washes, layered color, and stacked paper.

Murray's return to pure lithography in the early 1990s came with an intensity and excitement as her prints joined her paintings and entered the third dimension. *Shoe String*, 1993, was made from thirty-six aluminum plates and has twenty-one colors. Set against a richly worked palette of red and black, hand-torn sheets of paper, lightly washed in blue with accents of pink, curve outward, linked by a string woven through the elements. The image is printed on both sides, using the transfer press, resulting in a mirror image of the plate on the paper, and the handfed offset press, giving the exact image of the plate. Murray's next print *Shack*, 1994, combines techniques of *Shoe String* and the earlier dog prints, incorporating separate sheets of paper and three dimensional qualities, using 143 aluminum plates and twenty colors. Murray sees these prints as revelations. "*Shoe String* and *Shack* were really, for me, super provocative…they fed back into my paintings and gave me ideas. I could see how to work out my paintings inside my prints."

While Murray completed *Shack*, she began working on a set of mezzotints over monoprint with printers Lund and Lorena Salcedo-Watson. The artist and printers agree that these prints were an effort to do something more simply. The practice of mezzotint and the spontaneity of coloring the monoprint below the fixed, matrix print were very satisfying for Murray. Reminiscent of the physical and direct way she paints, Murray scraped, incised, and burnished away the surface of the copper plates to create her most recent prints, *Bedtime, Goodbye Girls*, and *Lovers*, 1996.

Robert Rauschenberg

Robert Rauschenberg had produced 78 editions at ULAE by 1982 and has made 27 more since, not including the numerous works made for philanthropic causes. Since 1960, when he teased Jasper Johns about "writing on rocks," Rauschenberg has been one of the world's most innovative printmakers, continually challenging the printers at ULAE with his mantra, "if you can think of it, you can do it."

ROBERT RAUSCHENBERG, CAPTIVA, FLORIDA, 1996.

In the early 1980s, Rauschenberg spent a great deal of time with printers at ULAE working out the continual technical details associated with the use of photography in his work. Editions such as *The Razorback Bunch I-VII*, 1980-83, and *Hoss, Faus, Glint*, and *Pre-Morocco*, all 1984, demonstrate the slow move from the half-tone process used in *Glacial Decoy Series*, 1979-80, to photogravure, which, with the use of random-pattern grain aquatint, produces a continuous tone resulting in rich, full color. A direct outcome of this experimentation was the *Bellini* series, begun in 1986 and completed in 1989, which consists of five very large prints, each made from between eight and eleven plates. The new and important technical challenge faced in this series was the replication of the surface crackle that Rauschenberg was using in his paintings at the time. Fortunately, printer Craig Zammiello was able to invent a solution that could be painted on a sheet of Lexan plastic on top of a printed proof; when the solution dried, it cracked and formed a surface texture that evokes his paintings.

Rauschenberg tends works in suites or series, each of which has a definite look that is different, new, and exciting. He completes a series only when his interest in it has been exploited or has dissipated, when he has found a solution and is once again free to work on another project. The *Bellini* series led directly into the seven *Soviet American Array* prints from 1988-91, a project that emerged from ROCI (Rauschenberg Overseas Culture Interchange), an evolving exhibition that presented the artist's response to varied cultures. He and his team of assistants visited Mexico; Chile; Venezuela; Tibet and Beijing, China; Japan; Cuba; the Soviet Union; Germany; Malaysia; and then the United States. He took photographs and gathered indigenous materials for his sculpture and paintings in all of these locations, and asked writers to contribute texts to accompany the work. Rauschenberg chose photographs from the Soviet Union for his print project with ULAE because of the rich history of printmaking in the Soviet Union and as a reaction to the sudden exchange of ideas between the Russians and the people of the United States.

Throughout the process of printing the editions Rauschenberg was in transit and carried on communication with ULAE when possible by mail, telephone or fax. Rauschenberg would send black-and-white negatives to ULAE, which the printers would then enlarge and return. He would, in turn, create collages and send them back with colors assigned. Photogravure plates were made and proofs were printed. When the proofs finally reached Rauschenberg and he approved them, the prints were editioned. As all of the other series laid groundwork for those which followed, so did this one.

The impetus for *Street Sounds*, 1992; *Street Sounds West*, 1993; and *Street Sounds East*, 1995, came from Rauschenberg's previous work with photogravure. But this series had an added twist: color. Goldston and the printers at ULAE were not sure if color photogravures could be made, but were willing to try. Color transparencies were made from slides that Rauschenberg had shot at various times, and were sent to him. He collaged the transparencies and returned them for ULAE to use as maquettes. Separating the colors, mixing the ink colors, using photogravure on copper plates, and calculating the stretch of the paper were all challenges that took a year to resolve. Rauschenberg describes the finished editions as "the result of some of the most absurd techniques and attempts and failures, always within an adventure." This spirit continues in his most recent series, *Ground Rules*, in which he, Zammiello, and Goldston have discovered yet another way to make gravure, allowing the artist to work directly on the plate, brushing developer on his image by hand and controlling its outcome.

JASPER JOHNS

Since the historic and well-documented moment when Jasper Johns first began working at ULAE in 1960, he has editioned more than 250 prints with various print studios. Across the close to forty years he has been working at ULAE, Johns has focused on mastering the various processes of printmaking. He has rarely explored imagery different from that of his paintings and drawings. Rather, he notes, "it's the printmaking techniques that interest me. My impulse to make prints has nothing to do with my thinking 'it's a good way to express myself.' It's more a means to experiment in technique."

Johns' technical innovation developed simultaneously with the growing capacity of ULAE. Today, Johns feels fortunate to have begun his printmaking journey with the most elemental of equipment, noting that "limited procedures make more interesting work." He believes that today's print world, with its sophisticated shops and teams of printers, can pressure an artist toward forms that are too elaborate.

JASPER JOHNS (LEFT) AND BILL GOLDSTON, ULAE STUDIO, 1996.

By 1982, twenty-two years after his first lithograph, Johns had become known as one of the masters of twentieth-century printmaking and had completed 76 editions including five portfolios at ULAE. Between 1982 and 1983, using the handfed offset press, Johns accomplished five more lithographs, based on *Voice 2*,

1971, a painting comprised of three 6-foot high canvases with superimposed stencil-style letters spelling "Voice 2." Similar to the painting, the first of the editions features three panels, offering the owner six possible visual sequences. As a continuation of his explorations with mixing transparent color with gray, as seen in *Voice 2*, Johns made *Ventriloquist*, 1985. Also based on a painting, this time only a fragment of the original, the print offers a reminder of past and a glimpse of future imagery,

incorporating the flags from his early works and introducing images drawn from George Ohr pots in his personal collection. In the following years, two more prints and a poster, used for his print retrospective at the Museum of Modern Art, would be editioned using the same title.

During the production of *Ventriloquist*, 1985, Arion Press asked Johns to illustrate a book containing the poems of Wallace Stevens. Inspired by Stevens' poem "The Snowman," two plates evolved, *Summer* and *Winter*. At the time of publication, *Summer* was in a more complete state than *Winter* and was therefore used as the frontispiece of the book. *Winter* was editioned and released the following year and the seeds were sown for his series of prints based on the four seasons. In 1987, ULAE published *The Seasons* (*Spring, Summer, Fall, Winter*), four color intaglios, from nineteen plates. Five editions followed as he continued to work within this theme for the next three years.

The publication of *The Seasons* in such varieties unleashed an avalanche of analysis, and much has been written about their iconography. The prints are equally complex technically as they are in subject matter. Johns worked closely with printer Lund first laying down sugar lift on the copper plates and then brush-

ing the spitbite over aquatint. As painting with acid is not an exact science, Johns relied on Lund's experience and intuition in determining tone and color depth. The results were outstanding and both the artist and the printer had a great sense of satisfaction upon their completion.

In the early nineties, Johns made three intaglios with various subject matter. *Untitled*, 1991, is a horizontal black-and-white print utilizing plates from *Land's End*, 1967, and *Untitled*, 1992, is a color print introducing the galaxy image and incorporating plates from *The Seasons*. *Green Angel*, 1991, is an independent print made from six copper plates representing a new image whose origin Johns still refuses to divulge. His following four lithographs, *After Holbein* from 1993-94, were taken from a poster promoting the Hans Holbein, the Younger, drawing exhibition at the Kunstmuseum Basel (1988). In his classical exploration of technique, Johns created a variety of different images using the same subject matter, a young nobleman with his lemur. The first image involves a variation of the cross-hatching seen in his work from the 1970s, the second incorporates a strip of wood grain similar to that seen in *Savarin*, 1977, and the fourth, the blended color roll seen in *Ruler* and *Pinion*, both 1966, and *Decoy I*, 1971. The third print explores a new technique for Johns, using both lithographic printing presses to achieve symmetry without actually having to duplicate the drawing.

In 1995, Johns changed medium as well as subject matter. For the first time, he began working with mezzotint. In mezzotint, the artist begins somewhat in reverse, with a fully textured plate, and then manually burnishes or erases the surface to make areas that won't take ink, effectively working from dark to light tones. Johns completed three images with this technique. Based on recent paintings, the imagery is taken from an article in *Scientific American* (April 1952) by child psychologist Bruno Bettelheim. Johns has since returned to lithography and traditional intaglio producing three more images within the last year.

JAMES ROSENQUIST

James Rosenquist has worked at ULAE since 1964 and has always shifted between intaglio and lithography, without a strong preference for one over the other. For him, the difference is poetic: "Lithography is like mountains and clouds and etching is like rivers and valleys."

After *Dog Descending a Staircase*, 1982, which used all of the presses available at ULAE, the etching press and both lithographic presses (transfer and handfed offset), came *Electrical Nymphs on a Non-Objective Ground*, 1984, a lithograph from sixteen plates. The challenge for both the artist and Goldston was finding a ground that was non-objective, without reflection, color or paper grain. Goldston suggested that they try printing on white Formica. For Rosenquist, it was the perfect solution. Technically it was equally perfect because the lithographic ink flawlessly printed the image of sharp slashes intersecting with fragments of women's faces.

JAMES ROSENQUIST, 1996.

Night Transitions, 1985, a lithograph from thirteen plates, filled with white and purple flowers set against a dark background and slashes similar to that of its predecessor, is Rosenquist's rendition of time unfolding. It is his interpretation of "women and flowers blooming at night," and refers to a form of entertainment indulged in during the 1920s and 30s, on the coastal islands off Florida: lacking electricity or radio, the islanders invited guests over for drinks and to watch a night flower bloom.

Meditating on the dispersal of energy and spirit as it is released from the body is the basis for the painting and print, *The Persistance of Electrons in Space*, 1987, the last to date made by Rosenquist at ULAE. "If we blow up the world," explains Rosenquist, "where do the spirits – or energy – of a billion people go? You have these persistent charges that are frantic to go somewhere." In this intaglio print, color is achieved by overlapping plates, not by printing numerous colors. Rosenquist prefers to mix colors himself, commenting that "Michelangelo used just eight colors."

THE NINETIES

By the late eighties Bill Jensen, Susan Rothenberg, Elizabeth Murray, Terry Winters, Carroll Dunham, Robert Rauschenberg, and Jasper Johns had become the core group of artists working at ULAE. As the next the decade approached, Goldston once again began to seek out younger artists.

JANE HAMMOND

Jane Hammond made her first prints in 1987 with an unsolicited grant she received while teaching at the Maryland Institute of Art. To her surprise she found printmaking much more interesting than she suspected and arranged to use the school's facilities to continue making prints. She was embarking on her third set of monoprints when Goldston contacted her. Having seen her first solo exhibition at Exit Art in New York in February 1989, Goldston arranged for a studio visit the following month and while there bought a number of her drawings. Then, when she returned from her third printmaking project with 100 monoprints – a combination of drawing, etching, and chine collé – he offered to sell some and give her the full proceeds. "I didn't even know how unusual an offer it was," says Hammond, "nobody else in the art world does charity work." Goldston eventually sold most of the monoprints, allowing Hammond to withdraw from teaching and devote herself solely to making art. At the same time, Goldston invited Hammond to ULAE.

JANE HAMMOND AND BILL GOLDSTON, ULAE STUDIO, 1996.

Hammond recalls, "I remember one of the first times I went out there, I spent the night in the house (Skidmore Place) and there was a book, around twenty years old, about successful and famous women and one of the chapters was on Tanya. So I read it and learned about this woman and how special she was. Then I stumbled across Calvin Tomkins' book and learned more on the profile of ULAE. Bill had never given me even a five minute lecture on what ULAE was about or how important it was." Although inexperienced at working with lithography, Hammond had grand ideas. Her first print published at ULAE *Presto*, 1991, was a lithograph and silkscreen with collage, made from fifteen aluminum plates and one silkscreen. The print looks deceptively straightforward (a buck emerging from a top hat), set against a patterned background, but the layering is as complex as her drawings and paintings. She spent a great deal of time with printers Douglas Volle and Salcedo-Watson working out ways to create the monkey pattern in the background from cotton batting and lace.

Hammond's next print, *Full House*, 1992-3, builds on the ideas first explored in *Presto*, but far exceeds the earlier work in concept, scale, and complexity. She wanted the print to be taller than she was – the idea originally stemming from a childhood height chart –

and to look dog-eared, as if it had been folded repeatedly like an old map. The background had to be uneven, stained, and faded, as if it were an object – perhaps a paper doll game – that had been played and abandoned by various people over time. Hammond started with the paper, folding it as tightly as possible, opening it up and refolding it, jumping on it, and otherwise distressing it as the printers prepared to put the sheet through the press with a copper plate covered with soft ground. The result was an etching of the paper itself, with all its folds, cracks, and creases. Hammond then proceeded to work on the background plates using such various materials such as leaves from the catalpa tree in front of the house on Skidmore Place, raisins, rosemary, fishnet stockings, and eggshells to create many layers, thus achieving the shadowy, stained effect she had hoped for. A house was eventually silkscreened onto the shifting ground of etching, which, while deconstructed, was the backbone of the print. The figures, printed on the handfed offset press, were then collaged to a number of locations chosen by Hammond with the implication that they created only one of the many possible arrangements.

The idea of making a print that was more an object than a piece of paper also informs *Clown Suit*, 1995. Hammond made thirteen suits as drawings, one of which became a prototype for the print. "I always wanted the *Clown Suit* to be a print," says Hammond, "If it's made out of cloth, it's just a clown suit. But here, with the printmaking context behind it, it becomes something else." First mentally taking apart the prototype, Hammond looked for ways to recreate her use of acrylic, graphite, rubber stamps, and Japanese paper within the print. The diverse solutions included dipping rubber stamps in tusche and stamping them on the lithographic plate, using a printing ink that mimicked graphite, and making a photo-silkscreen of collaged Japanese paper. The resulting thirteen sheets of printed paper were sewn together by Salcedo-Watson and Stacey Dunn, an intern from Oklahoma State University, as a statement about femininity, acknowledging and ultimately defying the notion that "sewing and making flowers and snowflakes are part of being a girl and not something expected in the work of a serious New York artist."

KIKI SMITH, ULAE STUDIO, 1991.

KIKI SMITH

Like Hammond, Kiki Smith had made her own prints before coming to ULAE. Although Goldston had been aware of Smith's art for some time, it was not until he saw her prints at the Brooklyn Museum print biennial that he sought her out. "I was really impressed with the quality of the work, where an artist does everything him or herself…Kiki seemed to be a person who worked with paper a lot, so it seemed natural to work with her."

Smith's work is about the body, so when she came to ULAE, Goldston instructed her to bring nothing but herself. Having no experience with lithography, her first print, *Untitled*, 1990, a lithograph from nine stones and one plate, therefore incorporated the only thing she knew how to use, her body. Xerox transfers of her own hair and an inked wig were run directly through the press, resulting in a print that enhanced Smith's theory that women's hair is loaded with religious, historical, and sexual connotations. Her next print, *Banshee Pearls*, 1991, a suite of Xerox transfers printed on twelve sheets of paper, is composed of images of Smith's face and head, mixed with skulls, hair, flowers, drips, and spots. The title comes from Celtic folklore

and memories of her family; a Banshee (something that Smith's father would call her) is said to be a female spirit that yells on the moors to warn of a coming death in the family. Smith's grandmother's name was Pearl. In trying to describe why she made a connection between the two memories when titling the piece, Smith says, "The sheets of paper are like a string of heads, a collar. Maybe they are the banshee pearls."

The following year was filled with a number of emotional and technical breakthroughs for the artist. Encouraged by Goldston to try drawing on a copper plate, Smith was forced to overcome her reservations about drawing, which she had avoided for over ten years. "I had felt really insecure about my drawing. But being there and being in such a nurturing environment, I went back to drawing and making portraits. It totally changed my life. It was one of the most significant times in my life where someone came and said they supported me and trusted me as an artist and that was very meaningful to me personally." With the full support of Goldston, Smith set to work drawing on a 4 x 6-foot plate that had been prepared for her by printers Lund and Hitoshi Kido. She laid down on the copper plate and had Lund trace her, then filled the figure in with imagined musculature. The resulting image, *Sueño*, 1992, features a flayed, sleeping figure (Smith) curled in a fetal position that Smith relates to her sister Beatrice who died of AIDS in 1988.

Worm, also 1992, builds on the imagery and techniques explored in previous prints but represents a major leap in her approach to printmaking, incorporating etching with collage. This time, the central image, a photograph of the artist – taken with infrared film to reveal the heat of the body – in a huddled, self-protective position, is placed in a rectangular box and set against black paper with crude diamond-shaped cut-outs. A wormlike figure made from pieced-together photographs of Smith's body, stretches across the print, while handcut paper flowers hang suspended from the bottom edge of the central rectangle.

Throughout her career, Smith has also explored the interior terrain of the body. *Kiki Smith 1993*, 1993, had its genesis years before when she made a silkscreen of intestines that she drew while looking at Japanese book on articulated muscles. Dissatisfied with the results, she shelved it until several years later when she was working at ULAE, and Goldston suggested that she try the image in etching. With the two-color intaglio, made from only two copper plates, she was able to achieve the desired effect of a dark, deeply rich shape floating against a washed, gestural background. "It worked," says Smith, "because of the surface achieved by acid etching."

Soon after her arrival at ULAE Smith began working with printer Zammiello, on a project involving photo assemblages recreating Smith's head. By 1995, they still had not found a way to make a print that satisfied Smith. In that year, Zammiello stumbled across a peripheral camera at the British Museum, its purpose being to take a cylindrical object and make it flat. Goldston and Zammiello proposed to Smith its possibilities related to their project and excited by the idea, made arrangements for the three of them to fly to England and for photographs to be taken of Smith. Upon their return, the resulting negatives were blown up and made into photogravures, then colored ink was added by Smith to the black inked photogravure plate for the red of the hair and the blue of the face, making

each version of the print unique. The final image, *My Blue Lake*, 1995, with Smith's head and upper body splayed like a topographical map, is haunting and stunningly beautiful. The completion of this print fulfilled a personal goal that Smith had when she first came to ULAE, which was to make a print of the skin of the body, laid out flat.

JULIAN LETHBRIDGE

Julian Lethbridge began working at ULAE in 1989. Well aware of its history, his greatest challenge became establishing a starting point beyond those of Johns and Rauschenberg. "In a way, it is much easier to make a print because you have their experience and insight. On the other hand, it is much harder. In a certain sense, an image and the relationship between the tusche and the stone could be quite sufficient for a print, but in 1995, it already looks like someone else's work."

Lethbridge began working on a stone using imagery he had been exploring in his drawings and paintings. Frustrated by the comparative flatness of the proofs that were pulled, and surprised and disappointed when the stone unexpectedly broke, Lethbridge and the printers looked for a way to save the image and create a more interesting surface to work with. Searching for a solution, printer Brintzenhofe ran a patched up version of Lethbridge's stone through the press with an aluminum plate, which embossed the stone into the plate. This created an echo of the stone, and when the plate was printed, a textural, ghost image of the stone on paper resulted.

Although this first image was never editioned, experimentation on it laid the groundwork for Lethbridge's first three published prints. For *Untitled*, 1990, and two prints called *Untitled* in 1991, Lethbridge surfaced a copper plate with open bite and etched it deeply with an image based on the wing of a caddis fly. The printers ran the etched plate through the press with an aluminum plate, producing a raised surface on the aluminum plate. Lethbridge then drew on this plate with tusche, circumventing the flatness the artist had found unsatisfactory.

For a time, Lethbridge had stopped using color in his paintings, drawings, and prints, feeling that black, white, and gray offered a "full range of rich possibilities." Slowly he reintroduced color into his prints, starting with *Chapel*, 1993, a two-color lithograph from two plates. Although the print appears black and white, it actually uses both green and red ink. The complimentary colors cancel each other out and move toward gray when surrounded by black; the result is an enhanced black tone.

Inspired by a mathematical problem, often referred to as the problem of the "traveling salesman," whose object it is to figure out how to connect a number of points and return to the original point using the shortest possible distance without intersecting lines, Lethbridge produced *Traveling Salesman*, 1995. A breakthrough for Lethbridge in many ways, it set a precedent for how he used individual colors on separate plates, as a key for making aesthetic decisions. "You do something on a plate," he says, "print it in black and then print it in color and you can completely isolate the impact of these different elements."

With this process, he was able to separate drawing from color, allowing him take advantage of the discrete spaces and simple structure the idea of the "traveling salesman" provided. Lethbridge was also able to overcome his frustrations with the limitations

JULIAN LETHBRIDGE, ULAE STUDIO, 1996.

of lithography – its flatness and permanence of the tusche once it was laid down on the stone or plate – by using Xerox toner suspended in alcohol. This material can be used for drawing, and can be manipulated and removed without leaving a lasting mark, thereby offering Lethbridge much greater flexibility.

SUZANNE MCCLELLAND

Suzanne McClelland came to ULAE with an excitement that was refreshing for everyone, especially McClelland. "Bill [Goldston] provided me with this play time and play space and people to work with that were really not only receptive, but there with – I hate to use the word technical – but physical solutions for things. And I never felt there was a barrier put up to, what I couldn't do."

With that enthusiasm, McClelland began and completed her first lithograph, *Then*, in 1993. Made from six aluminum plates and one silkscreen, it is a dense, layered print that used many elements from her paintings and drawings, including a newspaper background formulating a grid for the piece, and repeated words that form an abstract pattern.

Her subject is the opposition of impermanence of newsprint to the long-lasting impact of the written word. For her drawings she collects pages of the newspaper and uses them, not for collage, or in a cubist way, but by reading the page and noticing how the grid presents what is going on in the world.

Tea Leaves, 1996, a massive lithograph and silkscreen from fifteen plates and sixteen silkscreens, measuring 7 x 9 feet, is a continuation of this subject matter and an exploration of ideas begun in her paintings. Starting with one page from a newspaper, the piece continued to grow through the constant cutting, enlarging, and jumbling up of the page. The process of using one page from a newspaper over and over again, expanding it to its largest possible size, making it seem endless, reminded McClelland of the words "more" and "anymore" used in her paintings from the same time. As an extension of her interest in speech, dialogue, conversation, and the repetition within, McClelland incorporated the word "more" all over the print. McClelland's goal eventually became the creation of something that was "very large and very small at the same time." When viewed from a distance, it reads like a newspaper held at arms' length.

It took the printers as much time to figure out a way to print *Tea Leaves* as it did for McClelland to develop her ideas. Because the paper was too big to go through the press, the printers needed to find a way to take the image from the plates and transfer it to the paper. The solution they invented was to print the plates onto fusion glue, heat-affix the images to the paper, and then print the silkscreens on top. The result was a seamless ground with an encausticlike texture, reminiscent of her paintings, which combine gels, latex, and sometimes varnish.

The mechanical process and the transformation of the newspaper from something ordinary to something precious was crucial to the concept of both *Then* and *Tea Leaves*. This is also the case in her next suite of prints, *3:00, 6:00, 9:00, 12:00*, 1996, four color silkscreens made from the same page of newspaper that was the basis for *Tea Leaves*.

THE PAST AND FUTURE

The last fifteen years at ULAE have been marked by change and evolution, brought on not only by the

death of Tatyana Grosman but by the changing face of the art world. As a number of artists and printers who have spanned the decades at ULAE often remark, the romanticism and Old World idealism of the early years with Grosman gave way, out of necessity, to a professionalism and confidence that have supported the growth and status of the printshop.

Much of this was due to the remarkable period of expansion and activity under the leadership of Bill Goldston. Printmakers were hired, more sophisticated equipment acquired, and several offsite shops established. Twelve thoughtfully selected artists produced more than 200 prints, monotypes, and books between 1982 and 1997. The expanded range of equipment, particularly in the silkscreen and photogravure studios, has added to the artistic possibilities.

The sensibility that Grosman brought to ULAE has not been abandoned, however. That spirit still echoes through the modest structure in West Islip. Through forty years of rich creativity, the shop has led the renaissance of contemporary American printmaking, producing many of this century's finest prints.

True, Grosman is no longer there to charm the artists with tales of her days with Soutine and Picasso, tell stories of barely escaping Nazis, or dance at night when the fatigue of work became overwhelming. Her love for the process, absolute belief in the spirituality of what she was doing, and willingness to take on young artists have carried over from her era to the present. The vision and determination of Bill Goldston and the veteran artists and printers have sustained her memory through their work and their own dedication to quality and the necessity of experimentation.

For the artists and printers who never had the chance to meet Tatyana Grosman, her spirit still pervades. As Rauschenberg points out, "there is no pre-Tanya and post- Tanya. It's inseparable. She had such a strong, unforgettable, indelible sense of quality that we are all transfused and retransfused every minute. So she's there even though she's not there."

ENDNOTES

The quotes and information supplied by the artists and Bill Goldston in this essay were obtained during the following interviews:

CARROLL DUNHAM: *May 3, 1996.*

BILL GOLDSTON: *December 12, 1995, and February 9, 1996.*

JANE HAMMOND: *April 9, 1996.*

BILL JENSEN: *February 9, 1996.*

JASPERS JOHNS: *June 9, 1996.*

JULIAN LETHBRIDGE: *April 9, 1996.*

SUZANNE MCCLELLAND: *April 10, 1996.*

ELIZABETH MURRAY: *May 2, 1996.*

ROBERT RAUSCHENBERG: *June 5, 1996.*

JIM ROSENQUIST: *June 4, 1996.*

SUSAN ROTHENBERG: *June 17, 1996.*

KIKI SMITH: *April 14, 1996.*

TERRY WINTERS: *April 29, 1996.*

1983–1996

ARTISTS & WRITERS

Donald Baechler

Jim Dine

Carroll Dunham

Jane Hammond

Bill Jensen

Jasper Johns

Julian Lethbridge

Suzanne McClelland

Elizabeth Murray

Robert Rauschenberg

Larry Rivers

James Rosenquist

Susan Rothenberg

Joel Shapiro

Kiki Smith

Anne Waldman

Terry Winters

John Yau

PRINTERS

Shelly Beech

Doug Bennett

Keith Brintzenhofe

Thomas Cox

Richard Dawson

Bill Goldston

Hitoshi Kido

John Lund

Nancy Mesenbourg

Lorena Salcedo-Watson

Jihong Shi

Scott Smith

Douglas Volle

Bruce Wankel

Craig Zammiello

PLATE 73

JIM DINE
A Heart at the Opera, 1983
lithograph, 50 × 38 IN.

30/38 Larry Rivers '83

PLATE 74

LARRY RIVERS
Garbo Grosman, 1983
lithograph, 31 x 36 IN.

PLATE 75

SUSAN ROTHENBERG
Plug, 1983
lithograph, 30 x 22 IN.

PLATE 76

SUSAN ROTHENBERG
Between the Eyes, 1983–84
lithograph and woodcut with collage, 57 1/2 x 34 IN.

PLATE 77

SUSAN ROTHENBERG
Four Green Lines, 1984
lithograph, 30 1/2 X 35 IN.

PLATE 78

SUSAN ROTHENBERG
Missing Corners, 1984
monoprint, 24 × 15 1/2 IN.

A.P. 3/10   *Electrical Nymphs in a Non-Objective Ground*   James Rosenquist 1984

PLATE 79

JAMES ROSENQUIST
Electrical Nymphs on a Non-Objective Ground, 1984
lithograph, 42 X 42 IN.

PLATE 80

TERRY WINTERS
Morula I, 1983–84
lithograph, 41 3/4 x 31 5/8 in.

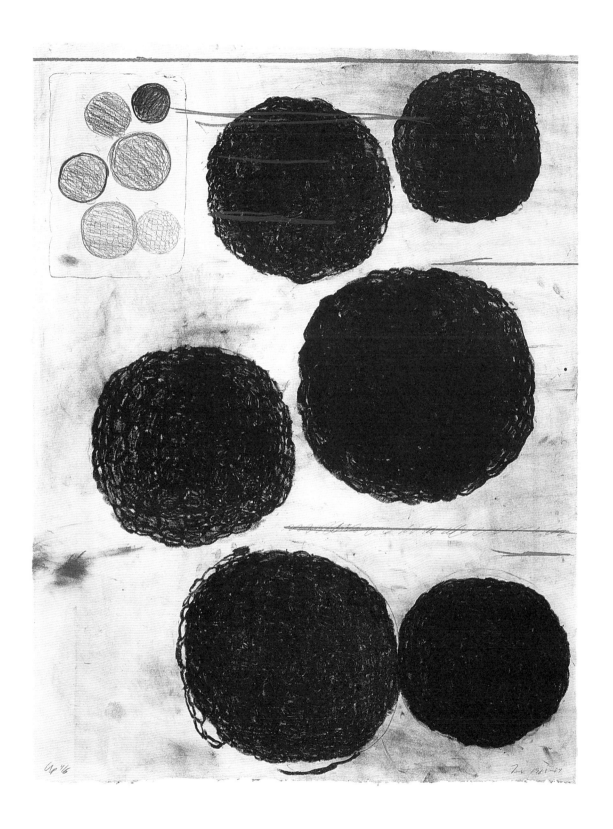

TERRY WINTERS

Morula II, 1983–84

lithograph, 42 1/4 x 32 1/2 IN.

PLATE 81

PLATE 82

TERRY WINTERS
Morula III, 1983-84
lithograph, 42 x 32 1/2 IN.

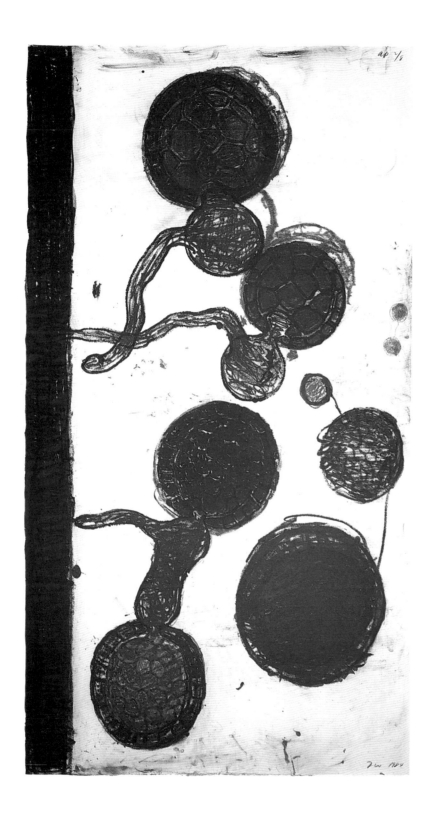

PLATE 83

TERRY WINTERS
Double Standard, 1984
lithograph, 78 x 42 in.

PLATE 84

PLATE 85

CARROLL DUNHAM
Accelerator, 1985
lithograph, 42 X 29 3/4 IN.

AP 4/10.   JS 85

PLATE 86

JOEL SHAPIRO
#1, 1985
wood collage, 17 x 13 1/2 IN.

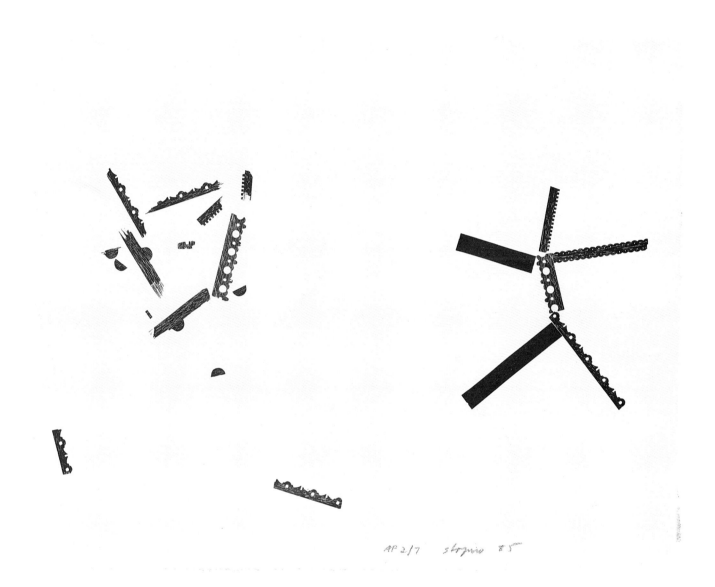

AP 2/7   shapiro 85

PLATE 87

JOEL SHAPIRO
#2, 1985
wood collage, 19 x 24 in.

PLATE 88

JOEL SHAPIRO
#3, 1985
wood collage, 17 x 13 1/2 IN.

PLATE 89

JASPER JOHNS
Ventriloquist, 1986
lithograph, 41 1/4 x 29 IN.

PLATE 90

ELIZABETH MURRAY
#1, 1986
lithograph, 22 x 31 IN.
Douglas and Leslie Volle

ROBERT RAUSCHENBERG

Bellini #1, 1986

intaglio, 58 1/4 x 38 1/4 IN.

PLATE 91

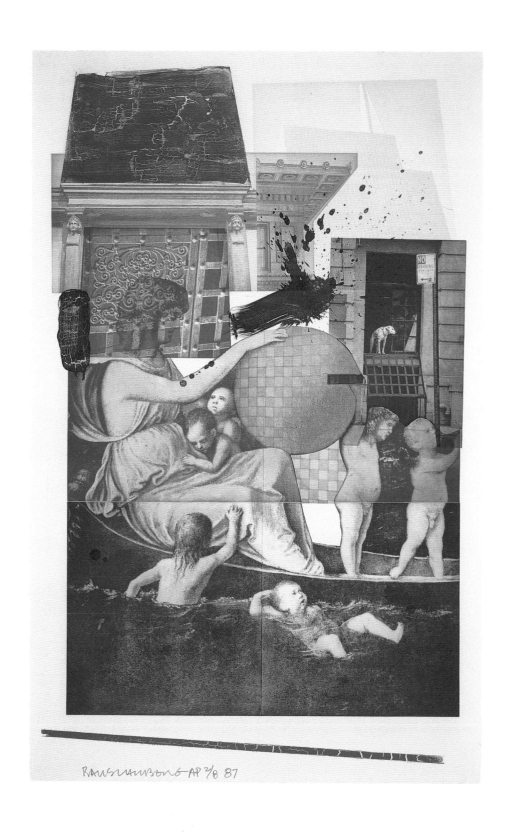

PLATE 92

ROBERT RAUSCHENBERG
Bellini #2, 1987
intaglio, 58 7/8 x 37 1/4 IN.

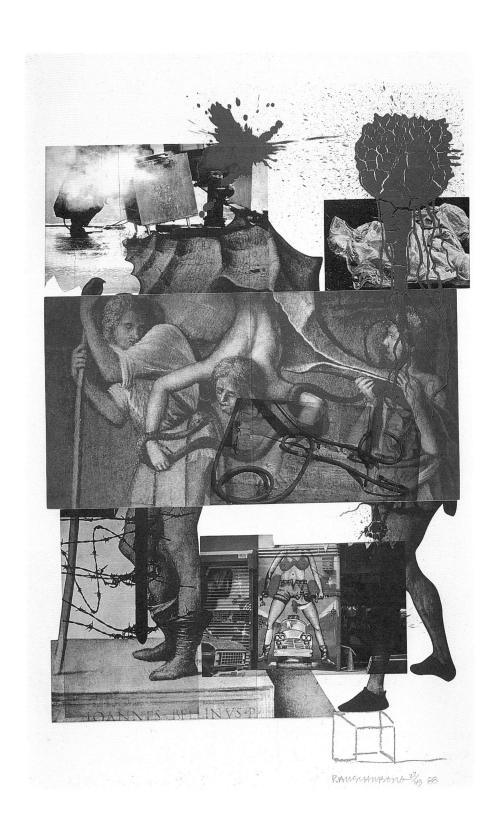

ROBERT RAUSCHENBERG
Bellini #3, 1988
intaglio, 59 x 37 1/2 IN.

PLATE 93

PLATE 94

ROBERT RAUSCHENBERG
Bellini #4, 1988
intaglio, 60 x 38 1/2 IN.

PLATE 95

Robert Rauschenberg
Bellini #5, 1989
intaglio, 59 x 38 1/4 in.

PLATE 96

Susan Rothenberg
Blue Violin, 1986
woodcut, 65 x 42 1/2 in.
Laura Burrows-Jackson, Baltimore, Maryland

PLATE 97

SUSAN ROTHENBERG
Stumblebum, 1985-86
lithograph, 86 1/2 x 42 1/2 in.

PLATE 98

TERRY WINTERS
Folio, 1986
unbound portfolio of lithographs, each sheet 31 x 22 1/2 IN.

CARROLL DUNHAM
Full Spectrum, 1985–87
lithograph with silkscreen, 42 x 28 IN.

PLATE 99

PLATE 100

JASPER JOHNS
The Seasons (Spring), 1987
intaglio, 26 x 19 IN.

63/73

PLATE 101

JASPER JOHNS
The Seasons (Summer), 1987
intaglio, 26 x 19 IN.

PLATE 102

PLATE 103

JASPER JOHNS
The Seasons (Winter), 1987
intaglio, 26 X 19 IN.

N° ?   *The Persistance of Electrons in Space*   *James Rosenquist 1987*

PLATE 104

JAMES ROSENQUIST
The Persistance of Electrons in Space, 1987
intaglio, 40 x 36 5/8 IN.
Craig and Lisa Zammiello

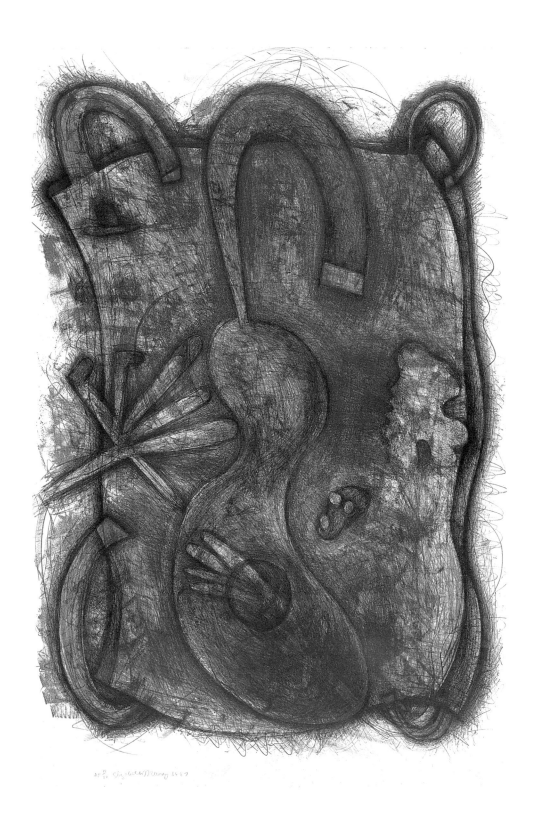

ELIZABETH MURRAY
Blue Body, 1986–87
lithograph, 47 3/4 x 31 5/8 IN.

PLATE 105

PLATE 106

SUSAN ROTHENBERG
Fish Sculpture, 1987
aluminum filled epoxy resin mounted on granite block, fish: 12 1/4 x 3 x 2 in., base: 8 1/2 x 5 x 5 in.

CARROLL DUNHAM
Red Shift, Red (1st), 1987–88
portfolio of lithographs, each sheet 30 x 22 1/2 IN.

PLATE 107

PLATE 108

BILL JENSEN
Babylon, 1985-88
intaglio, 20 x 15 in.

AP 4/7   Bill Jensen 1986-88

PLATE 109

BILL JENSEN
Etching for Denial, 1986 88
intaglio, 24 1/4 x 19 1/2 IN.

PLATE 110

ELIZABETH MURRAY
Up Dog, 1987–88
lithograph, 45 1/2 x 46 1/2 IN.

ELIZABETH MURRAY
Down Dog, 1988
lithograph, 50 3/4 x 41 in

PLATE 111

PLATE 112

CARROLL DUNHAM
Untitled, 1988–89
intaglio, 49 3/4 x 68 3/4 IN.

TERRY WINTERS
Marginalia, 1988
lithograph, 48 x 31 3/4 IN.

PLATE 113

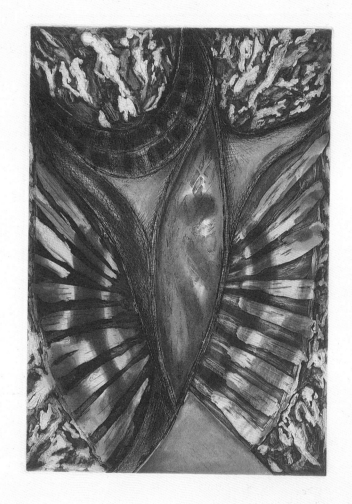

PLATE 114

BILL JENSEN
Vanquished, 1988–89
intaglio, 22 1/2 x 17 3/4 IN.

BILL JENSEN
Plight, 1985–89
intaglio, 20 X 15 1/4 IN.

PLATE 115

PLATE 116

JASPER JOHNS
Between the Clock and the Bed, 1989
lithograph, 26 1/4 X 40 1/4 IN.

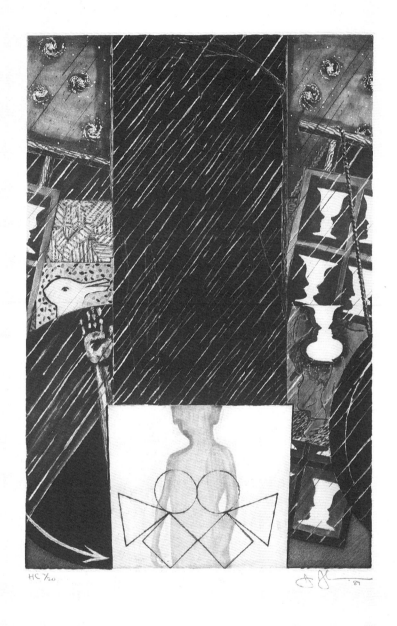

HC X/₂₀

PLATE 117

JASPER JOHNS
Spring, 1989
intaglio, 26 3/4 x 19 1/2 IN.

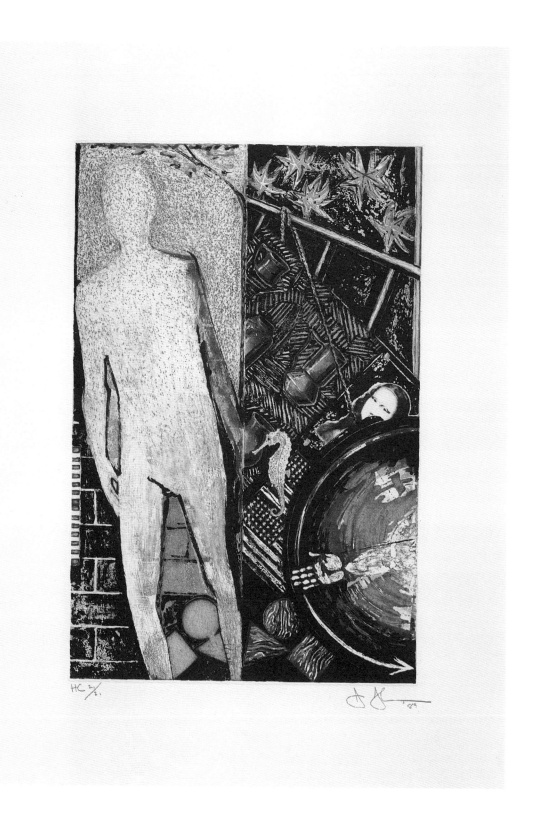

PLATE 118

JASPER JOHNS
Summer, 1989
intaglio, 26 3/4 X 19 1/2 IN.

HC 3/20

JASPER JOHNS
Fall, 1989
intaglio, 26 3/4 x 19 1/2 IN.

PLATE 119

PLATE 120

JASPER JOHNS
Winter, 1989
intaglio, 26 3/4 x 19 1/2 in.

PLATE 121

Robert Rauschenberg
Soviet/American Array I, 1988–89
intaglio, 88 1/2 x 53 1/2 IN.

PLATE 122

ROBERT RAUSCHENBERG
Soviet/American Array II, 1988–90
intaglio, 87 3/4 × 52 1/4 IN.

ROBERT RAUSCHENBERG

Soviet/American Array III, 1989-90

intaglio, 87 3/4 x 52 1/4 IN

PLATE 123

PLATE 124

ROBERT RAUSCHENBERG
Soviet/American Array IV, 1988–90
intaglio, 88 1/2 x 52 IN.

ROBERT RAUSCHENBERG
Soviet/American Array V, 1988–90
intaglio, 88 1/2 x 53 1/2 IN.

PLATE 125

PLATE 126

TERRY WINTERS
Fourteen Etchings, page ten, 1989
portfolio of intaglios, each sheet 18 5/8 x 14 1/8 IN.

TERRY WINTERS

Novalis, 1983–89

intaglio, 42 1/2 x 31 in.

PLATE 127

PLATE 128

BILL JENSEN
For Alice Too, 1990
intaglio, 21 x 20 3/4 IN.

PLATE 129

PLATE 130

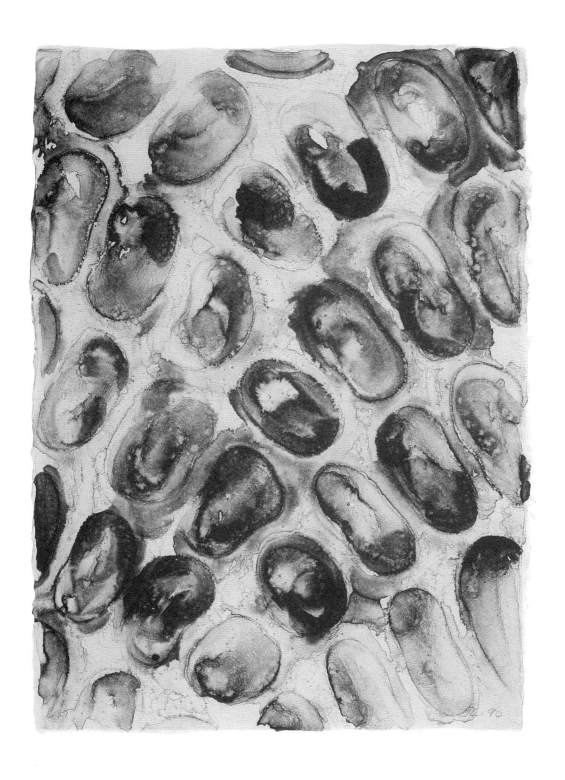

PLATE 131

JULIAN LETHBRIDGE
Untitled, 1990
lithograph, 22 3/4 X 17 IN.

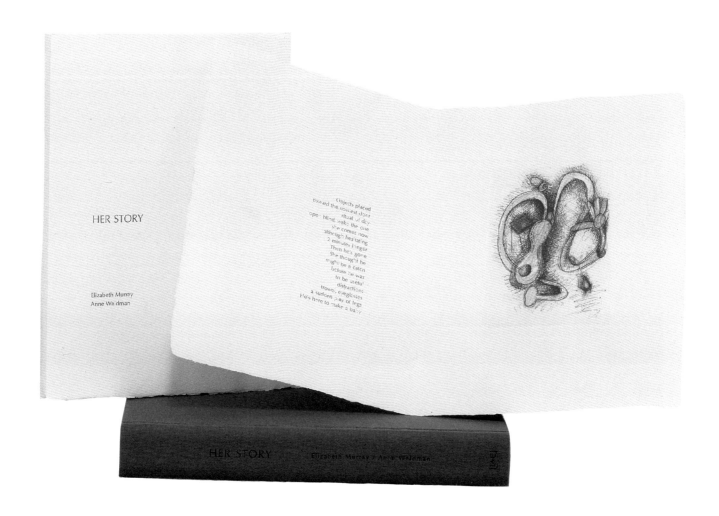

HER STORY

Elizabeth Murray
Anne Waldman

Objects placed
toward the noisiest door
ritual of day
open blind; wake the one
she comes now
although hesitating
2 minutes longer
Then he's gone
She thought he
might be a catch
before he was
to be useful
distractions
trowel, eyeglasses
a sudden play of legs
He's here to make a baby

HER STORY   Elizabeth Murray / Anne Waldman

PLATE 132

ELIZABETH MURRAY AND ANNE WALDMAN
Her Story, 1988–90
unbound book of lithographs with intaglios, each sheet 11 3/8 x 17 3/4 IN.

PLATE 133

ELIZABETH MURRAY
Undoing, 1989–90
lithograph and intaglio, 29 x 23 IN.

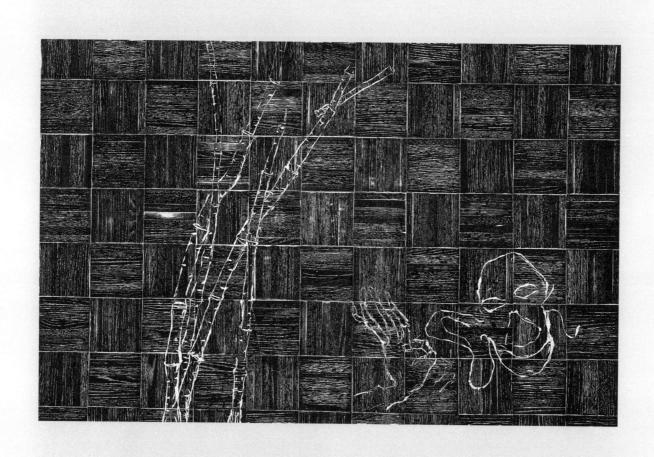

PLATE 134

SUSAN ROTHENBERG
Listening Bamboo, 1989-90
woodcut, 54 1/4 x 83 1/2 IN.

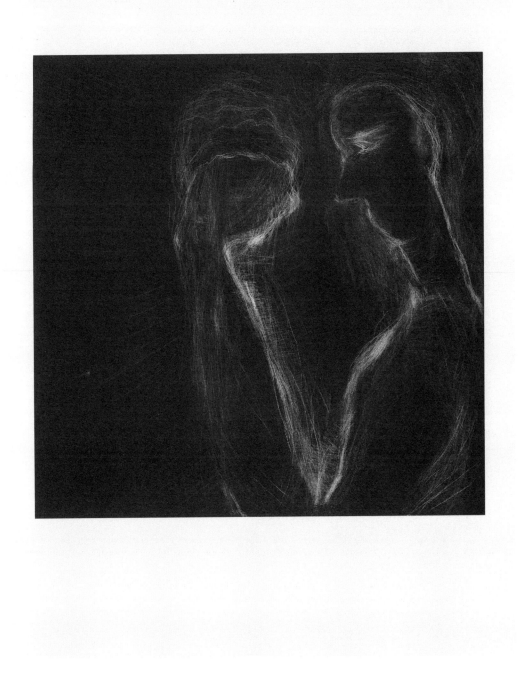

SUSAN ROTHENBERG
Mezzo Fist #1, 1990
mezzotint with collage, 31 x 22 1/2 IN.

PLATE 135

PLATE 136

KIKI SMITH
Untitled, 1990
lithograph, 36 x 36 IN.

PLATE 137

CARROLL DUNHAM
Analysis, 1991
wood engraving, 31 x 38 1/2 IN.

PLATE 138

BILL JENSEN
For Alice, 1990–91
intaglio, 22 1/2 x 21 3/4 IN.

PLATE 159

JANE HAMMOND

Presto, 1991

lithograph and silkscreen with collage, 39 3/8 x 25 5/8 IN.

PLATE 140

JASPER JOHNS
Untitled (Primaries with Secondaries), 1991
intaglio, 42 1/2 x 78 IN.

PLATE 141

JASPER JOHNS
Untitled, 1991
intaglio, 42 1/2 x 78 in.

PLATE 142

JULIAN LETHBRIDGE
Untitled, 1991
intaglio, 21 1/2 x 17 in.

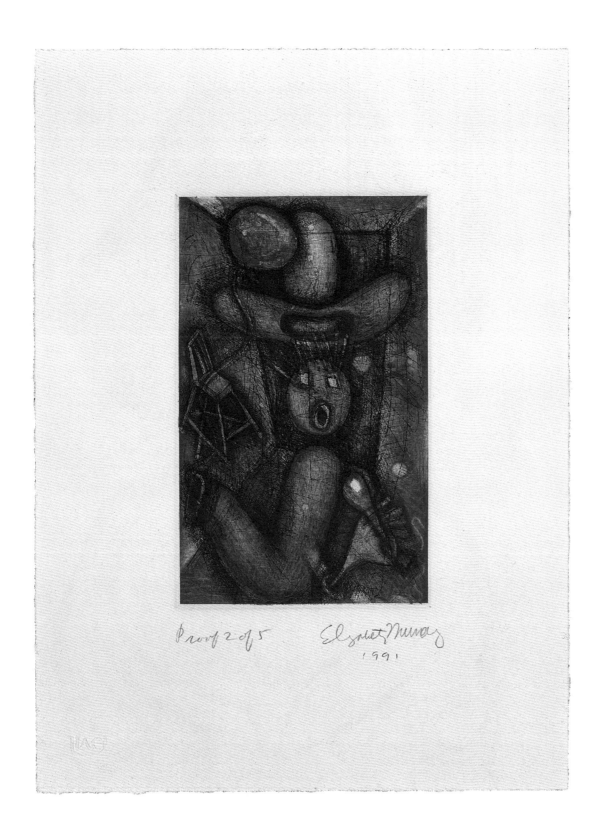

Proof 2 of 5   Elizabet Murray
                            1991

PLATE 143

ELIZABETH MURRAY
Hat, 1991
monotype over intaglio, 13 1/2 x 10 1/4 IN.

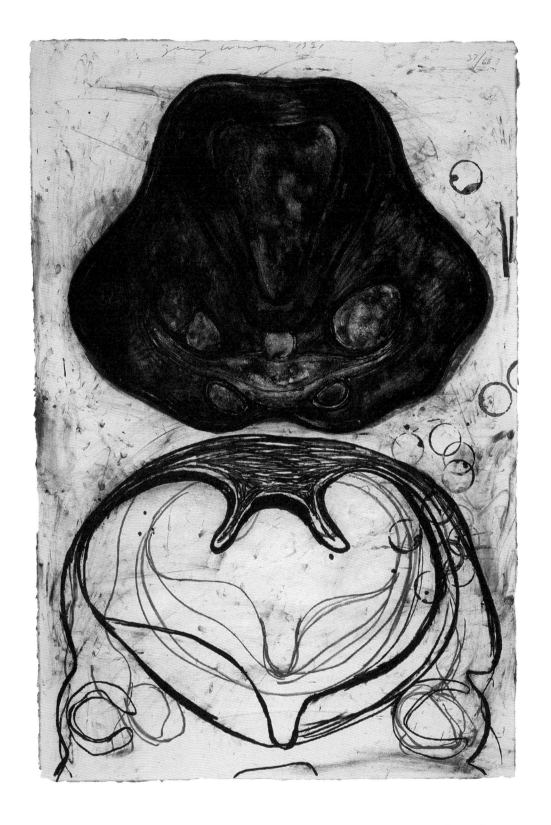

PLATE 144

TERRY WINTERS
Section, 1991
lithograph, 59 1/2 x 40 IN.

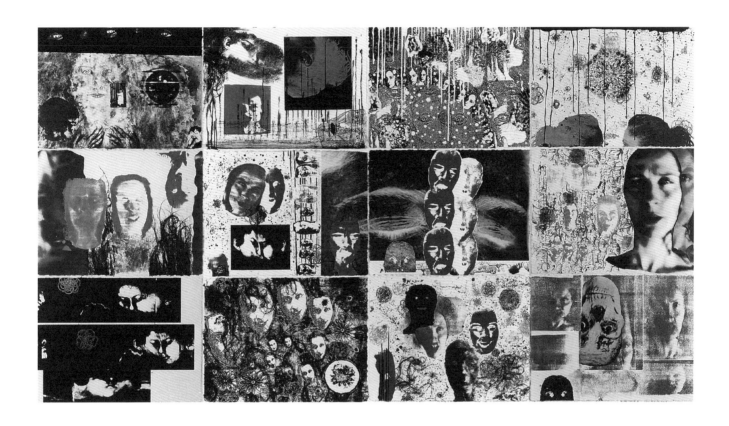

KIKI SMITH

Banshee Pearls, 1991
lithographs, each sheet 22 1/2 x 30 1/2 IN.
Dr. Robert and Mrs. Lisa Feldman

PLATE 145

PLATE 146

KIKI SMITH
Sueño, 1992
intaglio, 41 3/4 x 77 1/2 IN.

PLATE 147

KIKI SMITH
Worm, 1992
intaglio with collage, 42 x 62 IN.

PLATE 148

CARROLL DUNHAM
Point of Origin, 1988–92
intaglio, 49 1/4 x 68 3/4 IN.

PLATE 149

BILL JENSEN
Deadhead, 1991–92
intaglio, 21 3/8 x 19 IN.

PLATE 150

JASPER JOHNS
Untitled, 1992
intaglio, 43 1/2 X 52 1/2 IN.

ROBERT RAUSCHENBERG

Street Sounds, 1992

intaglio with photogravure and collage, 46 × 55 IN.

PLATE 151

PLATE 152

JULIAN LETHBRIDGE
Access, 1992
lithograph and silkscreen, 26 3/8 x 19 1/4 IN.

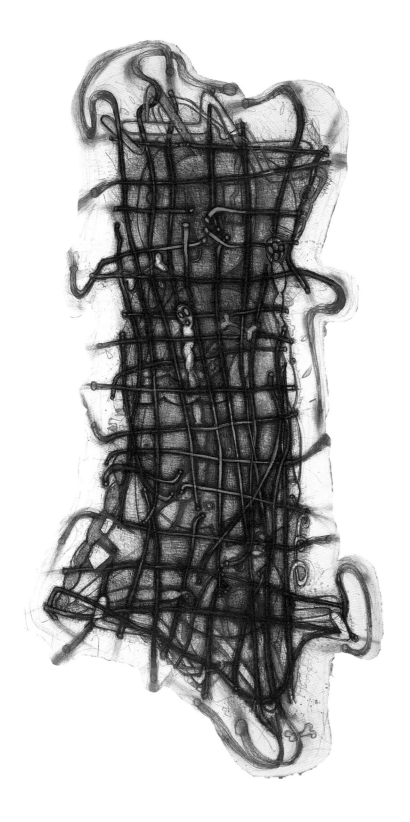

PLATE 153

ELIZABETH MURRAY
Wiggle Manhattan, 1992
lithograph, 58 3/4 x 29 IN.
Lorena and James Salcedo-Watson

PLATE 154

TERRY WINTERS
Theorem, 1992
lithograph, 31 3/4 x 48 1/8 IN.

PLATE 155

JULIAN LETHBRIDGE
Chapel, 1993
lithograph, 51 3/8 x 39 1/2 IN.

PLATE 156

JANE HAMMOND
Full House, 1992–3
intaglio and silkscreen with collaged lithographs, 78 1/2 X 51 IN.

PLATE 157

SUZANNE MCCLELLAND
Then, 1993
lithograph and silkscreen, 22 X 30 IN.

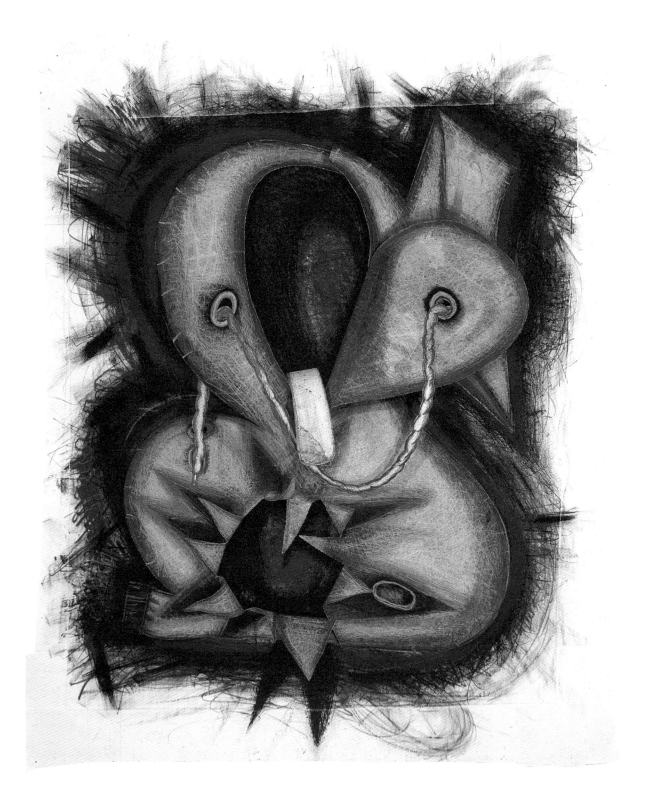

PLATE 158

ELIZABETH MURRAY
Shoe String, 1993
three-dimensional lithograph, 40 3/4 x 33 3/4 x 5 in.

KIKI SMITH
Kiki Smith 1993, 1993
intaglio, 73 x 36 1/2 in.

PLATE 159

PLATE 160

CARROLL DUNHAM
Seven Places, Alpha, 1990–94
portfolio of intaglios, each sheet 19 3/4 x 24 5/8 IN.

Postcard 16

Memory's branch quivers
beneath the weight of a butterfly

How am I to know what it wants
without asking

Could it be that simple, the question
and then the answer

Why do we fall outside of these additions
or consult the zodiac surrounding us

read its rotten walls and bulb glare
Why substitute names for things

when the things name us
(our vowels and consonants)

into their sleep,
one from which they will never awaken

Am I just an echo drifting back to myself
who is sitting beneath the river

drinking air
Something must have told me to say this

A rock or the memory of a rock
falling toward the shadow it once owned

BILL JENSEN AND JOHN YAU
Postcards from Trakl, 1989–94
book of intaglios and woodcut, book size 14 1/2 × 11 7/8 IN.

PLATE 161

PLATE 162

Elizabeth Murray
Shack, 1994
three-dimensional lithograph, 63 x 51 x 3 in.

PLATE 163

TERRY WINTERS
Models for Synthetic Pictures, #7, 1994
portfolio of intaglios, each sheet 19 3/8 x 22 1/4 IN.

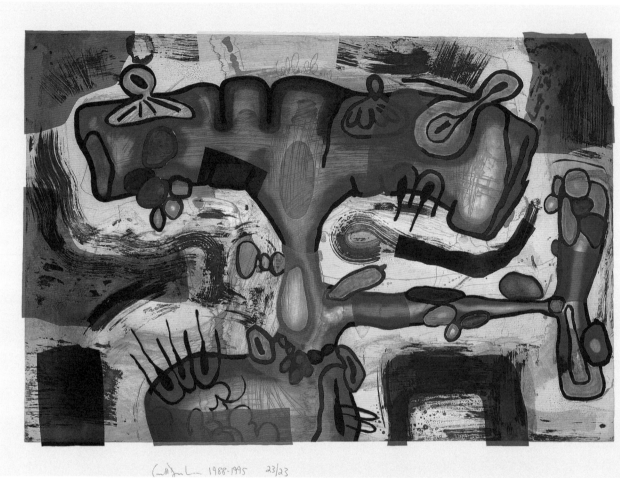

PLATE 164

CARROLL DUNHAM
Another Dimension, 1988–95
intaglio, 48 x 67 1/2 IN.
Dr. Robert and Mrs. Lisa Feldman

PLATE 165

JANE HAMMOND
Clown Suit, 1995
three-dimensional lithograph and silkscreen with collage, 55 x 39 x 10 IN.

PLATE 166

JASPER JOHNS
After Holbein, 1994
lithograph, 32 1/4 x 25 IN.

PLATE 167

JASPER JOHNS
Untitled, 1995
lithograph, 41 3/8 x 53 1/4 IN.
Jo Fielder

JASPER JOHNS
Untitled, 1995
mezzotint, 26 X 19 IN.

AP ⅗

PLATE 169

JASPER JOHNS
Untitled, 1995
mezzotint with drypoint, 29 3/4 X 22 1/2 IN.

10/39

PLATE 170

JASPER JOHNS
Untitled, 1995
mezzotint, 26 X 19 IN.

Julian Lethbridge
Untitled, 1995
lithograph, 33 1/4 x 27 in.
Doug and Cathleen Bennett

PLATE 171

PLATE 172

JULIAN LETHBRIDGE
Traveling Salesman, 1995
lithograph, 43 3/4 x 42 1/4 IN.

JULIAN LETHBRIDGE
Traveling Salesman, 1995
lithograph, 43 3/4 × 42 IN.

PLATE 173

PLATE 174

KIKI SMITH
My Blue Lake, 1995
lithograph with photogravure, 43 1/2 X 54 3/4 IN.
John and Christina Lund

PLATE 175

DONALD BAECHLER

The Two-Sided Flower, 1996
lithograph printed on both sides of sheet, 19 X 12 3/4 IN.

A.P. 3/6   *Lovers*   Elizabeth Murray 96

PLATE 176

ELIZABETH MURRAY
Lovers, 1996
mezzotint over monotype, 28 3/4 x 26 1/2 IN.

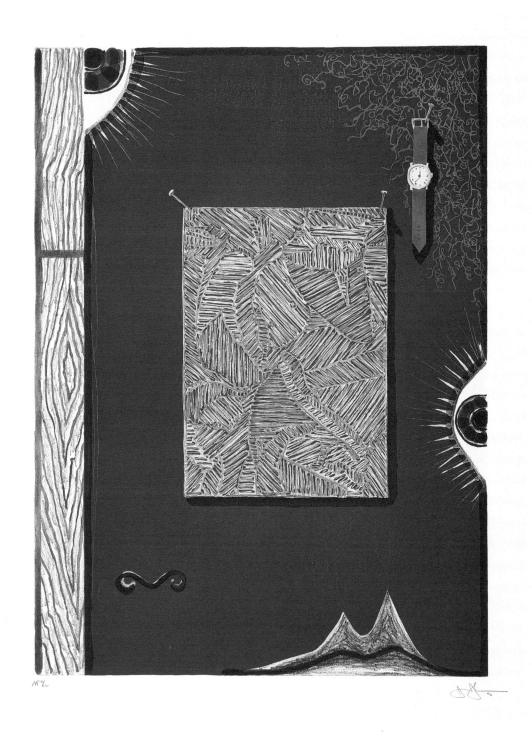

JASPER JOHNS
Face with Watch, 1996
intaglio, 42 × 31 7/8 IN.

PLATE 177

PLATE 178

BILL JENSEN
Lurisia, 1996
intaglio, 44 1/2 x 31 3/4 IN.

PLATE 179

BILL JENSEN
Defiance, 1996
intaglio, 36 1/4 x 42 3/4 IN.

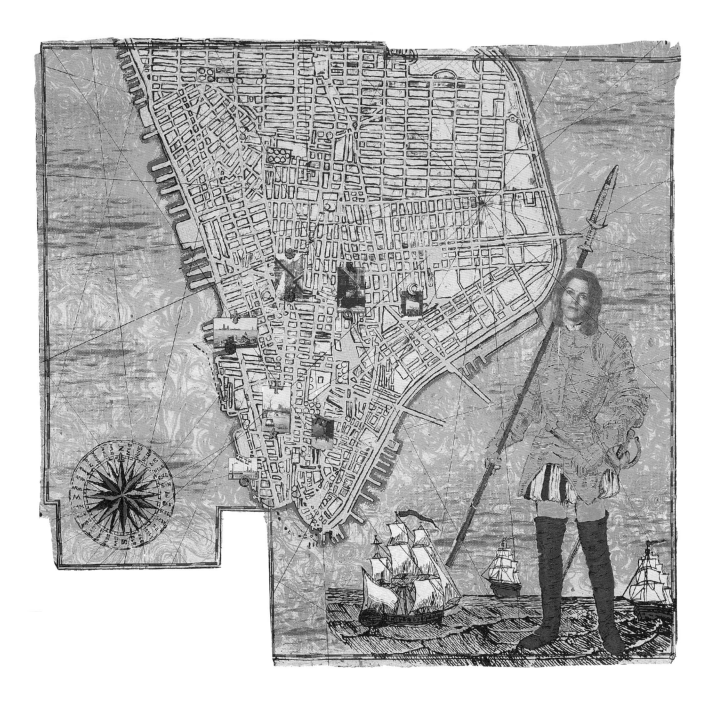

PLATE 180

JANE HAMMOND
The Wonderfulness of Downtown, 1996 – 7
trial proof   lithograph and silkscreen with collage, 59 1/2 x 62 in.

PLATE 181

SUZANNE MCCLELLAND
Tea Leaves, 1996
lithograph and silkscreen with collage, 86 x 108 IN.
Scott Smith

PLATE 182

TERRY WINTERS

Systems Diagram, 1996
intaglio, 42 X 50 IN.

PLATE 183

TERRY WINTERS
Untitled, 1996
lithograph, 33 3/4 x 48 IN.
Bruce and Marlene Wankel

PLATE 184

SUZANNE MᶜCLELLAND
3:00, 1996
lithograph and silkscreen, 47 1/4 x 31 1/2 IN.

SUZANNE MCCLELLAND

6:00, 1996

lithograph and silkscreen, 47 1/4 x 31 1/2 IN.

PLATE 185

PLATE 186

SUZANNE McCLELLAND
9:00, 1996
lithograph and silkscreen, 47 1/4 x 31 1/2 in.

SUZANNE McCLELLAND

12:00, 1996
lithographs and silkscreen, 47 1/4 x 31 1/2 IN.

PLATE 187

PLATE 188

ROBERT RAUSCHENBERG
Ground Rules (Intermission), 1996
intaglio, 63 x 51 3/4 IN.

ROBERT RAUSCHENBERG
Ground Rules (Banco), 1996
intaglio, 41 3/8 X 27 1/2 IN.

PLATE 189

TERRY WINTERS
Folio, 1986
portfolio of lithographs,
each sheet 31 X 22 1/2 IN.

Folio, title page
PLATE 190

Folio, One
PLATE 191

Folio, Two
PLATE 192

Folio, Three
PLATE 193

Folio, Four
PLATE 194

Folio, Five
PLATE 195

Folio, Six
PLATE 196

Folio, Seven
PLATE 197

Folio, Eight
PLATE 198

Folio, Nine
PLATE 199

Folio, colophon page
PLATE 200

CARROLL DUNHAM
Red Shift, 1987-88
portfolio of lithographs,
each sheet 30 X 22 1/2 IN.

Red Shift, Blue (2nd)
PLATE 201

Red Shift, Purple (3rd)
PLATE 202

Red Shift, Green (4th)
PLATE 203

Red Shift, Black (5th)
PLATE 204

TERRY WINTERS
Fourteen Etchings, 1989
portfolio of intaglios,
each sheet 18 5/8 X 14 1/8 IN.

Fourteen Etchings, page one
PLATE 205

Fourteen Etchings, page two
PLATE 206

Fourteen Etchings, page three
PLATE 207

Fourteen Etchings, page four
PLATE 208

Fourteen Etchings, page five
PLATE 209

Fourteen Etchings, page six
PLATE 210

Fourteen Etchings, page seven
PLATE 211

Fourteen Etchings, page eight
PLATE 212

Fourteen Etchings, page nine
PLATE 213

Fourteen Etchings, page eleven
PLATE 214

Fourteen Etchings, page twelve
PLATE 215

Fourteen Etchings, page thirteen
PLATE 216

Fourteen Etchings, page fourteen
PLATE 217

CARROLL DUNHAM
Seven Places, 1990-94
portfolio of intaglios,
each sheet 19 3/4 X 24 5/8 IN.

Seven Places, Beta
PLATE 218

Seven Places, Gamma
PLATE 219

Seven Places, Delta
PLATE 220

Seven Places, Epsilon
PLATE 221

Seven Places, Zeta
PLATE 222

Seven Places, Eta
PLATE 223

TERRY WINTERS
Models for Synthetic Pictures, 1994
portfolio of intaglios,
each sheet 19 3/8 X 22 1/4 IN.

Models for Synthetic Pictures, #1
PLATE 224

Models for Synthetic Pictures, #2
PLATE 225

Models for Synthetic Pictures, #3
PLATE 226

Models for Synthetic Pictures, #4
PLATE 227

Models for Synthetic Pictures, #5
PLATE 228

Models for Synthetic Pictures, #6
PLATE 229

Models for Synthetic Pictures, #8
PLATE 230

Models for Synthetic Pictures, #9
PLATE 231

Models for Synthetic Pictures, #10
PLATE 232

Models for Synthetic Pictures, #11
PLATE 233

Models for Synthetic Pictures, #12
PLATE 234

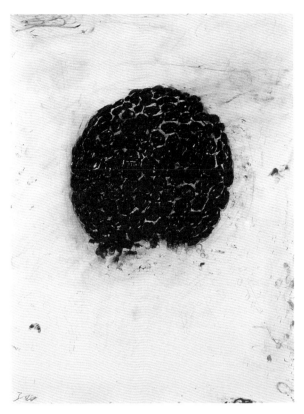

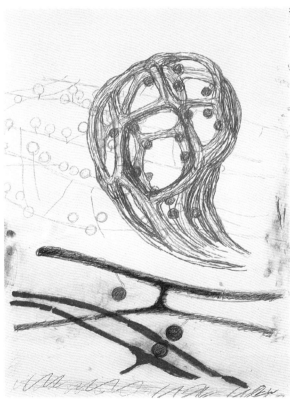

PLATE 190
PLATE 191

PLATE 192
PLATE 193

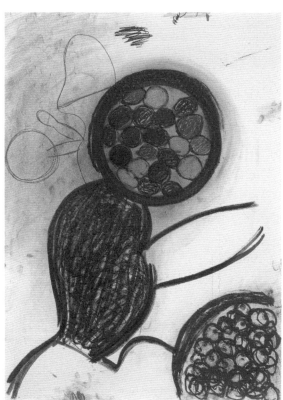

PLATE 194
PLATE 195

PLATE 196
PLATE 197

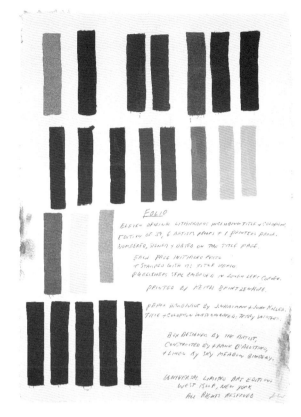

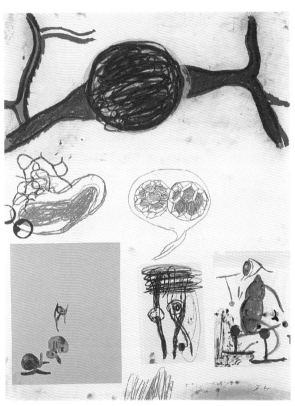

PLATE 198
PLATE 199

PLATE 200

PLATE 201
PLATE 202

PLATE 203
PLATE 204

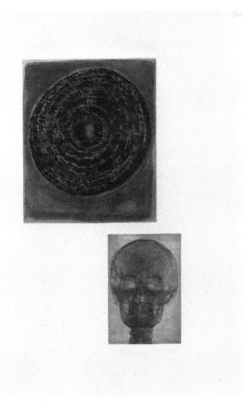

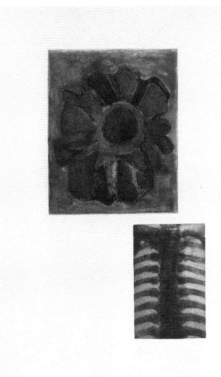

PLATE 205
PLATE 206

PLATE 207
PLATE 208

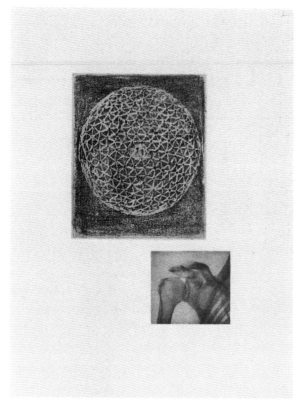

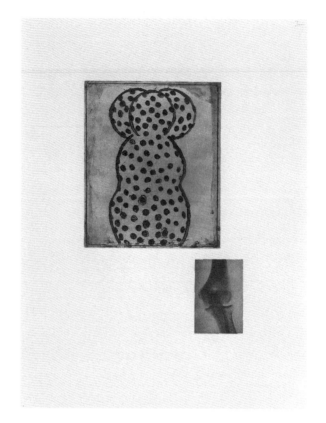

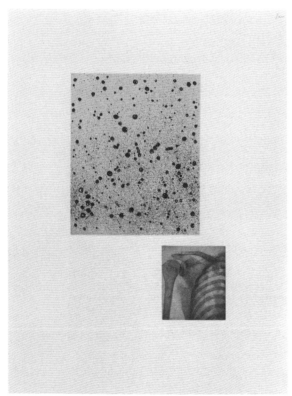

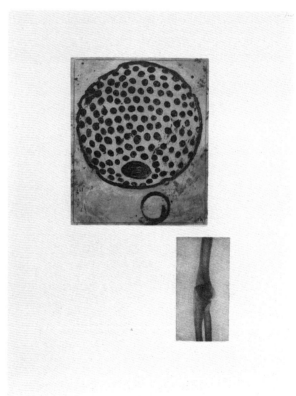

PLATE 209
PLATE 210

PLATE 211
PLATE 212

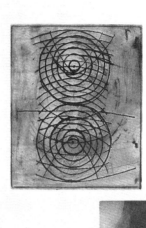

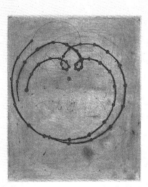

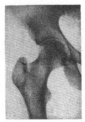

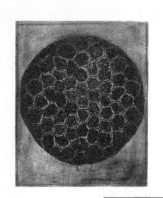

PLATE 213
PLATE 214

PLATE 215
PLATE 216

PLATE 217

PLATE 218
PLATE 219
PLATE 220

PLATE 221
PLATE 222
PLATE 223

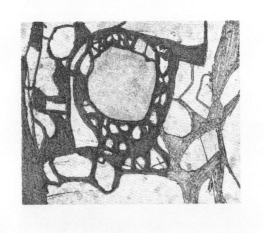

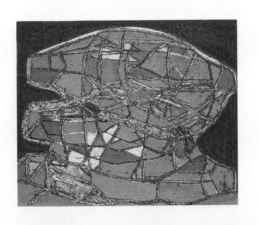

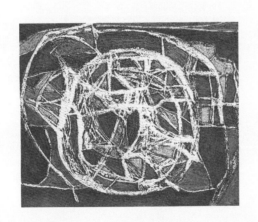

PLATE 224
PLATE 225
PLATE 226

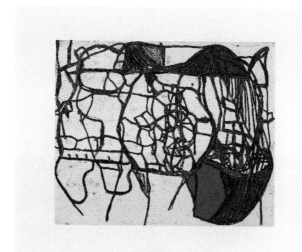

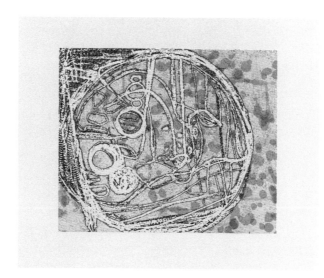

PLATE 227
PLATE 228
PLATE 229

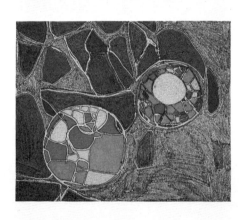

PLATE 230
PLATE 231
PLATE 232

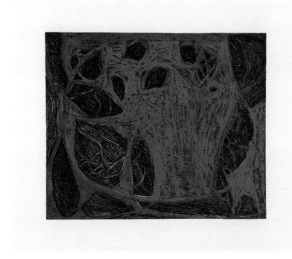

PLATE 233
PLATE 234

Descriptive Checklist

The descriptive checklist is comprised of biographies of the artists in the exhibition, listed in alphabetical order, with each biography followed by an exhibition checklist of that artist's works, listed in chronological order. This checklist documents the presentation of prints and books in *Proof Positive: Forty Years of Contemporary American Printmaking at ULAE, 1957-1997* at the Corcoran Gallery of Art, Washington, DC. The travelling version of this show will not be significantly changed, but some variations will occur because of the length of the tour, the fragility of works on paper, and the production of new editions by ULAE in 1997 and 1998.

The checklist entries for each print, book, portfolio or suite include the title, date, medium, production process, sheet dimensions, edition number, related proofs and lender to the Corcoran Gallery of Art presentation. The works are dated according to the artists' designations. Sheet dimensions are in inches, height by width by depth. The edition number indicates the size of the commercial edition. For editions and related proofs the following abbreviations are used:

AP Artist's proof of edition
CP Cancellation proof, with plate or stone and subsequent single printing marked to document cancelled state
HC *Hors commerce*, not for commercial distribution
PP Printer's proof
TP Trial proof
WP Working proof

Unless otherwise noted, all works are lent courtesy of Universal Limited Art Editions.

Biographies: Sue Scott

Catalogue data: Laura Coyle, Larissa Goldston

DONALD BAECHLER
B. 1956

Donald Baechler studied at the Maryland Institute College of Art (1974-1976), attended Cooper Union in New York (1977-1978), and Frankfurt's Staatliche Hochschule für bildende Künste (1978-1979). He has exhibited his paintings, drawings, prints, and sculpture internationally since having his first one-person show at the Maryland Institute College of Art in 1977. Baechler's work was included in the Whitney Museum of American Art's *Biennial Exhibition* (1989) as well as the Corcoran Gallery of Art's *43rd Biennial Exhibitions of Contemporary American Painting* (1994).

Baechler places crudely rendered line drawings of men, women, body parts, vegetables or flowers against richly built up backgrounds of paint, pentimenti and collaged sheets of paper. Like Jean Dubuffet's *l'art brut*, Baechler is inspired by the immediacy and spontaneity of the untrained artist: the art of the insane, children's school work, and graffiti. But while his interest in tapping subconscious urges through odd juxtapositions of seemingly unrelated images or objects links him to the Surrealist tradition, his interest in painterly, textured surfaces is closer in spirit to abstract artists such as Cy Twombly or Robert Ryman. Baechler began working at ULAE in 1995 at the invitation of Bill Goldston. Bypassing the compressed flatness that is a natural result of the printing process, his collage-based layering processes translate well into a wide variety of print media.

DONALD BAECHLER

The Two-Sided Flower, 1996
lithograph printed on both sides of sheet from four aluminum plates,
19 x 12 3/4 IN.
Edition 17, AP 5, PP 3
see plate 175

LEE BONTECOU
B. 1931

In 1957, two years after studying at the Art Students League (1952-1955), Lee Bontecou was awarded consecutive Fulbright Fellowships; these grants enabled her to spend two full years studying and working in Rome. In 1959, she received a Louis Comfort Tiffany Award; the following year she received the first of four solo shows at the Leo Castelli Gallery. Bontecou's work was included in the Corcoran Gallery of Art's *28th Biennial Exhibition of Contemporary American Painting* (1963), and has been featured in many prestigious national and international exhibitions, including surveys at London's Tate Gallery (1964) and The Art Institute of Chicago (1967).

Tatyana Grosman invited Bontecou to make lithographs for ULAE after viewing her 1962 Leo Castelli Gallery exhibition, which prominently featured the artist's drawings. Bontecou's first lithograph, aptly-named *First Stone*, 1962, reveals tentative explorations of the same imagery – textured, loosely fragmented gestural shapes encircling a void or hole – that she had created in her drawings and sculpture. Her explorations with lithography and etching continued at ULAE until the early 1980's.

LEE BONTECOU
Fourth Stone, 1963
lithograph from two stones,
41 1/2 x 29 5/8 IN.
Edition 19, AP 2
*Robert and Jane Meyerhoff, Phoenix,
Maryland, see plate 9*

LEE BONTECOU
Seventh Stone, 1965-68
lithograph from one stone,
24 7/8 x 19 7/8 IN.
Edition 31, AP 4, pp 1
see plate 35

LEE BONTECOU AND TONY
TOWLE
Fifth Stone, Sixth Stone, 1967-68
six intaglios from six copper plates,
each sheet 20 x 26 1/4 IN.
Unbound book in a hand made paper
folder in a cloth covered wood box.
Edition 33, AP 7, pp 2
see plate 34

LEE BONTECOU
Fourteenth Stone, 1968-72
lithograph from two stones,
28 x 39 3/4 IN.
Edition 17, AP 3, pp 1
see plate 46

LEE BONTECOU
An Untitled Print, 1981-82
lithograph from 14
aluminum plates,
93 x 42 IN.
Edition 14, AP 5, pp 3
see plate 70

JIM DINE
B. 1935
Jim Dine graduated with a BFA
from the University of Ohio in
1958 and moved to New York
the following year. Almost
immediately, he met Allan
Kaprow, and by 1960 had staged
a number of happenings, among
them the influential *Car Crash.*
He also began painting and
drawing tools, articles of cloth-
ing, and household objects as
surrogates for himself. Success
came quickly, and by 1962 Dine
had been included in the

Pasadena Museum of Art's
influential *New Paintings of
Common Objects,* had joined the
prestigious Martha Jackson
Gallery, and had been featured
in a *Life Magazine* article profil-
ing 100 influential young
American men and women.
That same year Jasper Johns and
Robert Rauschenberg introduced him to Tatyana Grosman,
and the two felt an immediate
rapport.

Completed in 1962, Dine's
first prints depicted tools and
domestic items rendered in a
loose fashion that reflected his
affinity with the gestures of the
abstract expressionists. The 1962
lithograph *Eleven Part Self
Portrait (Red Pony),* which was
printed from two stones, was
the first of many featuring an
image of the artist's bathrobe as
an autobiographical surrogate.
In 1975, Dine began publishing
his own prints and since then
has returned only occasionally
to work at ULAE.

JIM DINE
Eleven Part Self Portrait (Red Pony),
1964-65
lithograph from two stones,
41 1/4 x 29 5/8 IN.
Edition 13, AP 2
Carol and Morton Rapp, see plate 19

JIM DINE
Boot Silhouettes, 1965
lithograph from one stone,
41 1/2 x 29 7/8 IN.
Edition 20, AP 1
Peter and Susan Ralston, see plate 17

JIM DINE
Double Apple Palette with Gingham,
1965
lithograph from 15 stones with
gingham collage,
23 1/4 x 28 IN.
Edition 23, AP 4
Peter and Susan Ralston, see plate 18

JIM DINE
2 Hearts (The Donut), 1970-72
diptych lithograph from 12 stones
and eight aluminum plates,
54 x 63 1/2 IN.
Edition 17, AP 4, pp 1
Nancy and Tom Driscoll, see plate 47

JIM DINE
A Heart at the Opera, 1983
lithograph from one stone
and eight aluminum plates,
50 x 38 IN.
Edition 50
see plate 73

CARROLL DUNHAM
B. 1949
After attending Trinity College
in Hartford, Connecticut,
Carroll Dunham moved to
New York in the early 1970s. He
began making abstract paintings
with an aesthetic that sought
inspiration not from the domi-
nant minimalist ethos, but from
surrealism, abstract expression-
ism, and pop art. From them he
gleaned a desire to tap into the
subconscious, a need to mine
the emotional power of color,
and the freedom to assimilate
aspects of popular culture into
his work. He had his first one-
person exhibition in New York
at Artists Space in 1981 and his
paintings have twice been featured in the Whitney Museum
of American Art's *Biennial
Exhibition* (1985 and 1995).

Dunham's references to art
history are subtly filtered
through memory and association. His high-key, often day-
glo colors bring to mind cartoons and album covers of the
1960s, while the biomorphic
forms that recur throughout his
work – the wave, the mound,
genitalia, tongue, and teeth –
satisfy the subconscious urges of
a child's doodling. As a result,
Dunham's prints, like his paint-

ings, function on many levels. A
single polymorphous shape may
simultaneously suggest the
internal meanderings of the
body's structure, a topographical
landscape, or an abstract maze.
Invited by Bill Goldston to
print at ULAE in 1984, Dunham's experiments with lithography resulted in *Accelerator,*
1985 which accomplished the
artist's penchant for dense layer-
ings of abstract imagery though
a succession of four lithographic stones.

CARROLL DUNHAM
Untitled, 1984-85
lithograph from two stones,
28 x 19 IN.
Edition 42, AP 6, pp 1
see plate 84

CARROLL DUNHAM
Accelerator, 1985
lithograph from four stones
and two aluminum plates,
42 x 29 3/4 IN.
Edition 51, AP 8, pp 1
see plate 85

CARROLL DUNHAM
Full Spectrum, 1985-87
lithograph from six stones with
silkscreen from seven screens,
42 x 28 IN.
Edition 68, AP 15, pp 3
see plate 99

CARROLL DUNHAM
Red Shift, 1987-88
five lithographs from 18 stones
and 22 aluminum plates,
each sheet 30 x 22 1/2 IN.
Portfolio in a folder.
Edition 49, AP 10, pp 2
see plates 107, 201-204

CARROLL DUNHAM
Another Dimension, 1988-95
intaglio from eight copper plates,
48 x 67 1/2 IN.
Edition 23, AP 7, pp 4
*Dr. Robert and Mrs. Lisa Feldman,
see plate 164*

CARROLL DUNHAM
Point of Origin, 1988–92
intaglio from two copper plates,
49 1/4 x 68 3/4 IN.
Edition 30, AP 11, pp 3
see plate 148

CARROLL DUNHAM
Untitled, 1988–89
intaglio from one copper plate,
49 3/4 x 68 3/4 IN.
Edition 53, AP 9, pp 4
see plate 112

CARROLL DUNHAM
Wave, 1988–90
intaglio from four copper plates,
53 x 73 1/2 IN.
Edition 43, AP 9, pp 2
see plate 130

CARROLL DUNHAM
Seven Places, 1990–94
seven intaglios from four
copper plates,
each sheet 19 3/4 x 24 5/8 IN.
Portfolio in a folder.
Edition 25, AP 5, pp 3 on 2 prints,
pp 2 on 5 prints
see plates 160, 218–223

CARROLL DUNHAM
Analysis, 1991
wood engraving from four
woodblocks, 31 x 38 1/2 IN.
Edition 38, AP 6, pp 2
see plate 137

HELEN FRANKENTHALER
B. 1928
Helen Frankenthaler studied
with Rufino Tamayo at the
Dalton School, graduating in
1945. By 1949, when she graduated from Bennington College, and
moved to New York to study at
Columbia University, she had
removed any trace of representation from her art, embracing
the philosophy of Clement
Greenberg, who believed that
modernism was taking abstraction toward anti-illusionistic flatness. Frankenthaler had her first
one-person exhibition at Tibor
de Nagy Gallery in 1951; she was

just twenty-three years old when,
in 1953, she painted *Mountains
and Sea,* her first abstract stain
painting. Success for her fresh
approach included first prize at
the biennial exhibition of the
Musée d'Art Moderne de la Ville
de Paris (1959), and traveling ret-
rospectives organized by the
Whitney Museum of American
Art (1969) and the Corcoran
Gallery of Art (1975).

At the suggestion of Larry
Rivers, Frankenthaler was invited
to work at ULAE in 1960 and
the lithography stone quickly
became a perfect vehicle for her
athletic brand of gestural abstraction. For the next fifteen years,
Frankenthaler continued her
fruitful collaboration at ULAE,
adding intaglio (1968) and woodcut (1973) to her repertoire.

HELEN FRANKENTHALER
First Stone, 1961
lithograph from five stones,
22 1/4 x 29 7/8 IN.
Edition 12, AP 2
*Mr. and Mrs. Sheldon Soffer, Teaneck,
New Jersey, see plate 5*

HELEN FRANKENTHALER
Persian Garden, 1965–66
lithograph from three stones,
25 3/4 x 20 IN.
Edition 24, AP 1
Lent by the artist, see plate 24

HELEN FRANKENTHALER
A Slice of the Stone Itself, 1969
lithograph from two stones,
19 x 15 IN.
Edition 24, AP 4, pp 2
Lent anonymously, see plate 40

HELEN FRANKENTHALER
Lot's Wife, 1970–71
triptych lithograph from
three stones,
137 5/8 x 36 3/4 IN.
Edition 17, AP 4, pp 1
see plate 41

HELEN FRANKENTHALER
East and Beyond, 1972–73
woodcut from eight lauan
mahogany plywood blocks,
31 7/8 x 22 IN.
Edition 18, AP 6
Carol and Morton Rapp, see plate 52

HELEN FRANKENTHALER
Savage Breeze, 1974
woodcut from eight lauan
mahogany plywood blocks,
31 1/2 x 27 1/4 IN.
Edition 31, AP 4, pp 3
see plate 53

R. BUCKMINSTER FULLER
1895-1983
Buckminster Fuller is best
known as the architect who
invented the geodesic dome, but
his diverse interests encompassed
art, sailing, and scientific theory.
His restless energy also worked
against him; he was twice
expelled from Harvard University, and spent much of his
career moving from one govern-
ment or corporate position to the
next. His appetite for work is evi-
denced in his penchant for public lectures lasting up to ten
hours, twenty-six patents, and
forty-three honorary degrees.

Fuller was eighty years old
in 1975, when Edwin Schlossberg
introduced him to Tatyana
Grosman over tea. Fuller described his great enthusiasm for a
project based on the tetrahedron
that would unify his ideas of
time, physics, synergy and the
cosmos. Mrs. Grosman was
intrigued, and committed Fuller
to work on a lithographic stone,
the first of many in the massive,
two-year *Tetrascroll* production
process. More than thirty feet in
length, this three-dimensional
"book" was composed of twenty-one lithographs divided into
twenty-six sections, each of
which formed an equilateral tri-

angle. Connected at the base, the
entire structure was designed to
be displayed freestanding. While
Tetrascroll provided a platform for
Fuller's wide ranging inventive-
ness, it also marked an engineer-
ing breakthrough for ULAE
printers, who found the means
to give three-dimensional form
to Fuller's ideas.

R. BUCKMINSTER FULLER
Tetrascroll, 1975–77
21 lithographs from 25 stones and
27 aluminum plates bound with
Dacron polyester sailcloth,
each sheet 35 1/2 x 35 1/2 x
35 1/2 IN.
Book of twenty-six sections, each
an equilateral triangle, with text,
title, preface, and colophon pages,
and epilever by Edwin Schlossberg.
Edition 34, AP 6, pp 2
see plate 63

FRITZ GLARNER
1899-1972
Born in Switzerland and educat-
ed at the Reggio Instituto di
Belle Arti in Naples (1914-1920),
Fritz Glarner did not make his
first abstract painting until he was
thirty-one. After this conversion,
however, he became a lifelong
devotee of geometric abstraction.
During a stay in Paris (1932-1935)
he joined the Abstraction-
Création group; after he immigrated with his wife to New York
in 1936, he became a member of
American Abstract Artists. Building on the tenets of de Stijl, su-
prematism, and the paintings of
Mondrian, Glarner developed his
own theory of abstraction, which
he called Relational Painting.
This theory simplified color use
to blue, yellow, red, and gradations of gray; textural differences
to slight gradations, and composition to forms suggested by the
trapezoid.

Glarner and his wife came to America as war refugees, and settled on Long Island. With their similar experiences and shared interests in contemporary art, they became good friends with Tatyana and Maurice Grosman, and in 1958 Glarner was invited by the Grosmans to print at ULAE. He completed nine black-and-white lithographs during the following year, and in 1963 he turned to color lithography, producing *Color Drawing for Relational Painting* and *Colored Drawing*. Glarner continued making prints, incorporating his theories of abstraction, texts from earlier exhibitions, with drawings for his Time-Life Building and United Nations Building commissions and observations about art and life until 1968 when he suffered brain injuries and was unable to continue making prints.

FRITZ GLARNER
Colored Drawing, 1963
lithograph from six stones,
24 3/4 X 20 IN.
Edition 23, AP 2
see plate 10

FRITZ GLARNER
Recollection, 1964-68
14 lithographs from 60 stones,
each sheet 14 3/4 X 23 IN.
Portfolio with title, preface, and colophon pages in a wood box with a hand-blown glass disk set into cover.
Edition 30, AP 6, pp 2
see plate 36

JANE HAMMOND
B. 1950
Jane Hammond studied poetry and biology at Mt. Holyoke College in Massachusetts before earning her BA in art. After studying ceramics at Arizona State University, Tempe, she received her MFA in sculpture from the University of Wisconsin at Madison (1979). She moved to New York and began compiling images from instructional or scientific manuals, children's books, books on puppetry and magic, as well as charts on alchemy, animals, religion, and phrenology. From this collection she culled 276 images which functioned as her image bank for subject matter.

In 1989 Hammond received her first one-person exhibition at the New York alternative space Exit Art; that same year, she received grants from the National Endowment for the Arts, the Louis Comfort Tiffany Foundation, and the New York State Council on the Arts. Since 1989, Hammond has exhibited internationally in Sweden, Milan, and Holland. Her work has been the subject of one-person exhibitions at the Honolulu Academy of Arts, the Cincinnati Art Center, and the Orlando Museum of Art. Hammond was invited by Bill Goldston to print at ULAE in 1989; after experimenting with monoprints, she turned to a combination of lithography, silkscreen, intaglio, and collage to achieve the complex layering of her trademark images.

JANE HAMMOND
Presto, 1991
lithograph from 15 aluminum plates and silkscreen from one screen with collage,
39 3/8 X 25 5/8 IN.
Edition 48, AP 13, pp 2
see plate 139

JANE HAMMOND
Full House, 1992-93
intaglio from six copper plates and silkscreen from six screens with collaged lithographs from 31 aluminum plates,
78 1/2 X 51 IN.
Edition 32, AP 4, pp 6
see plate 156

JANE HAMMOND
Clown Suit, 1995
three-dimensional lithograph from 42 aluminum plates and silkscreen from six screens with collage,
55 X 39 X 10 IN.
The suit was machine stitched with cotton/poly thread by Lorena Salcedo-Watson and Stacey Dunn. The "pom-poms" are hand-stitched paper and attached with stainless steel hardware.
Edition 45, AP 10, pp 3
see plate 165

JANE HAMMOND
The Wonderfulness of Downtown, 1996-7
lithograph and silkscreen with collage,
59 1/2 X 62 IN.
TP
see plate 180

GRACE HARTIGAN
B. 1922
Grace Hartigan studied with Isaac Lane Muse in New York (1942-1947); by 1949, after spending a year in Mexico, she returned to New York and began to paint abstractly. She was quickly accepted into a circle that included Mark Rothko, Jackson Pollock, Adolph Gottlieb, and Willem de Kooning, and exhibited with them in the *9th Street Show.* She was included in *Talent: 1950,* organized by Meyer Schapiro and Clement Greenberg for the Kootz Gallery, and in 1951 she held the first of seven exhibitions with Tibor de Nagy Gallery. Hartigan's work has been featured in the Whitney Museum of American Art's *Annual Exhibition* (1955), the São Paulo *Biennale* (1957), and *Documenta* (1959).

Hartigan was a maverick: until 1953 she signed her paintings as George Hartigan, both in homage to George Sand and George Eliot, and to make a point about the sexism of the art world. Stylistically restless, she shifted between representation and abstraction. Hartigan made several screenprints for the magazine *View,* and collaborated with the poet James Schuyler on *Salute,* 1960, published by Tiber Press. That same year, at the suggestion of Larry Rivers, she began working at ULAE, creating four black-and-white lithographs inspired by the Barbara Guest poem "The Hero Leaves His Ship." Following her only color lithograph, *Pallas Athene* (1961), Hartigan again took Guest's work as her point of departure for the *Archaics* Series, published in 1966.

GRACE HARTIGAN
The Hero Leaves His Ship IV (Ship), 1960
lithograph from one stone,
21 1/8 X 29 3/4 IN.
Edition 28
*Laura Burrows-Jackson,
Baltimore, Maryland*

GRACE HARTIGAN
The Archaics: Atalanta in Arcadia, 1962-66
lithograph from one stone,
27 1/2 X 19 7/8 IN.
Edition 20, AP 1
see plate 25

GRACE HARTIGAN
The Archaics: From Eyes Blue and Cold, 1962-66
lithograph from one stone,
27 1/2 X 19 7/8 IN.
Edition 20, AP 1
see plate 26

GRACE HARTIGAN
The Archaics: In the Campagna,
1962–66
lithograph from one stone,
27 1/2 x 19 7/8 IN.
Edition 20, AP 1
see plate 27

BILL JENSEN
B. 1945
Bill Jensen received his MFA in
1970. The following year he
moved to New York, where his
large-scale abstract paintings
involved images of spirals and
ellipses on surfaces made of a
mixture of synthetic varnish,
hand-ground pigments, oil, and
sand. However, a toxic reaction
to his materials forced him to
abandon painting for a year;
upon resuming a full-time studio practice, he conceived the
intimately scaled abstractions for
which he is well known. Jensen
has been preoccupied with an
eclectic mix of stylistic predecessors that include Albert
Pinkham Ryder, Marsden
Hartley, Arthur B. Dove, and
Francisco Goya.

Jensen had his first show at
the Fishbach Gallery in New
York (1981), and the same year
was included in the *Biennial Exhibition* at the Whitney Museum
of American Art. He has been a
part of *Five Painters in New York*
(1984) the *Fortieth Biennial of
Contemporary American Painting*
(1987), at the Corcoran Galley of
Art, and his work was the subject of a retrospective organized
by the Phillips Collection in
Washington, DC (1987) In 1986
he received a fellowship from
the National Endowment for
the Arts.

Jensen was one of the first
artists invited by Goldston to
print at ULAE. Beginning in

1983, he explored all avenues of
intaglio technique, using his talent to make twenty-one editions
to date.

BILL JENSEN
Babylon, 1985–88
intaglio from five copper plates,
20 x 15 IN.
Edition 50, AP 8, pp 2
see plate 108

BILL JENSEN
Plight, 1985–89
intaglio from four copper plates,
20 x 15 1/4 IN.
Edition 50, AP 8, pp 2
see plate 115

BILL JENSEN
Etching for Denial, 1986–88
intaglio from one copper plate,
24 1/4 x 19 1/2 IN.
Edition 51, AP 7, pp 3
see plate 109

BILL JENSEN
Vanquished, 1988–89
intaglio from five copper plates,
22 1/2 x 17 3/4 IN.
Edition 53, AP 10, pp 3
see plate 114

BILL JENSEN
Lie-Light, 1989–90
intaglio from six copper plates,
18 1/4 x 23 IN.
Edition 55, AP 10, pp 3
see plate 128

BILL JENSEN AND JOHN YAU
Postcards from Trakl, 1989–94
12 intaglios from 12 copper plates
and woodcut from one woodblock,
book size 14 1/2 x 11 7/8 IN.
Book with 22 poems by John Yau
with title, colophon, and dedication pages in a box.
Edition 75, AP 10, pp 5
see plate 161

BILL JENSEN
For Alice, 1990–91
intaglio from seven copper plates,
22 1/2 x 21 3/4 IN.
Edition 45, AP 13, pp 3
see plate 138

BILL JENSEN
For Alice Too, 1990
intaglio from seven copper plates,
21 x 20 3/4 IN.
Edition 51, AP 11, pp 2
see plate 129

BILL JENSEN
Deadhead, 1991–92
intaglio from seven copper plates,
21 3/8 x 19 IN.
Edition 41, AP 11, pp 4
see plate 149

BILL JENSEN
Defiance, 1996
intaglio from six copper plates,
36 1/4 x 42 3/4 IN.
Edition 32, AP 7, pp 2
see plate 179

BILL JENSEN
Lurisia, 1996
intaglio from four copper plates,
44 1/2 x 31 3/4 IN.
Edition 34, AP 6, pp 1
see plate 178

JASPER JOHNS
B. 1930
Jasper Johns moved to New York
in 1949 and began paintings
influenced by abstract expres-
sionism.

Introduced to Robert Rau-
schenberg, John Cage, and
Merce Cunningham in the mid-
1950s, his work changed radical-
ly. The first of many one-person
exhibition at Leo Castelli Gallery (1958) led to his inclusion
the following year in the
Museum of Modern Art's land-
mark *16 Americans.* One-person
exhibitions of his paintings,
drawings, prints, and sculpture
have been organized by the
Whitney Museum of American
Art (1977), the National Gallery
of Art (1990), and the Museum
of Modern Art (1986, 1996).

With Rauschenberg, Jasper
Johns stands as an important
bridge between abstract expres-
sionism and pop and minimal

art. Printmaking has long been
an important part of the process
of both artists. Johns has created
over 250 prints and print editions, working with such promi-
nent ateliers as Gemini G.E.L.,
Simca Print Artists, and
Petersburg Press. He first worked
at ULAE in 1960, after Tatyana
Grosman, with Rauschenberg's
help, carried three lithographic
stones up four flights of stairs to
his studio. Initially, lithography
suited Johns and enabled him to
create print versions of the iconic depiction of flags, maps, and
targets that filled his paintings,
such as *Target,* 1960. In 1967,
Johns expanded his repertoire to
etching and created *Target I* and
Light Bulb. In 1971, Johns became the first artist at ULAE to
use the handfed offset lithographic press, resulting in *Decoy*
— an image realized in printmaking before it was made in
drawing or painting. Since then,
Johns has become a master of
both media and continues making prints with subjects as varied
as the seasons, creative reinter-
pretations of Holbein, and curious faces and features combined
with everyday objects.

JASPER JOHNS
0-9 B/C, 1960–63
10 lithographs from three stones,
each sheet 20 1/2 x 15 1/2 IN.
Portfolio with title and colophon
pages, and an introduction by
Robert Rosenblum, in a linen
folder in a wood box.
Edition 10, AP 3
see plate 11

JASPER JOHNS
Flag I, 1960
lithograph from one stone,
22 1/4 x 30 IN.
Edition 23, AP 3
Tony and Gail Ganz, see plate 2

JASPER JOHNS
Target, 1960
lithograph from one stone,
22 1/2 x 17 1/2 IN.
Edition 30, AP 3
Jane Fearer Safer, see plate 3

JASPER JOHNS
False Start I, 1962
lithograph from 11 stones,
31 1/2 x 22 1/2 IN.
Edition 38, AP 6
Private Collection, see plate 6

JASPER JOHNS
False Start I, 1962
lithograph with chalk,
31 1/2 x 22 1/2 IN.
WP 5
*Private Collection, Baltimore,
Maryland*

JASPER JOHNS
Ale Cans, 1964
lithograph from seven stones,
22 1/2 x 17 1/2 IN.
Edition 31, AP 2
*Private Collection, Courtesy of
the Thomas Segal Gallery, Baltimore,
Maryland, see plate 15*

JASPER JOHNS
Decoy, 1971
lithograph with die cut from one
stone and 18 aluminum plates,
41 x 29 IN.
Edition 55, AP 4, pp 4
Brian Goldston, see plate 42

JASPER JOHNS
Scent, 1975-76
3 panel print with left panel: lithograph from four aluminum
plates, center panel: linocut from
four linoleum blocks, and right
panel: woodcut from four woodblocks,
31 1/4 x 47 IN.
Edition 42, AP 7, pp 3
Renie and Stan Helfgott, see plate 62

JASPER JOHNS
Usuyuki, 1980
lithograph from 13
aluminum plates,
52 1/2 x 20 1/4 IN.
Edition 57, AP 11, pp 3
see plate 66

JASPER JOHNS
Voice 2, 1982
three-panel lithograph from
20 aluminum plates,
each sheet 35 3/4 x 24 1/4 IN.
Edition 54, AP 5, pp 4
Lent Anonymously, see plate 71

JASPER JOHNS
Ventriloquist, 1986
lithograph from 11 aluminum
plates,
41 1/4 x 29 IN.
Edition 69, AP 15, pp 1
see plate 89

JASPER JOHNS
The Seasons (Spring), 1987
intaglio from five copper plates,
26 x 19 IN.
Edition 73, AP 16, pp 4
see plate 100

JASPER JOHNS
The Seasons (Summer), 1987
intaglio from five copper plates,
26 x 19 IN.
Edition 73, AP 14, pp 4
see plate 101

JASPER JOHNS
The Seasons (Fall), 1987
intaglio from five copper plates,
26 x 19 IN.
Edition 73, AP 14, pp 4
see plate 102

JASPER JOHNS
The Seasons (Winter), 1987
intaglio from four copper plates,
26 x 19 IN.
Edition 73, AP 13, pp 4
see plate 103

JASPER JOHNS
Between the Clock and the Bed, 1989
lithograph from ten
aluminum plates,
26 1/4 x 40 1/4 IN.
Edition 50, AP 8, pp 3
see plate 116

JASPER JOHNS
Spring, 1989
intaglio from one copper plate,
26 3/4 x 19 1/2 IN.
HC 20
see plate 117

JASPER JOHNS
Summer, 1989
intaglio from one copper plate,
26 3/4 x 19 1/2 IN.
HC 21
see plate 118

JASPER JOHNS
Fall, 1989
intaglio from one copper plate,
26 3/4 x 19 1/2 IN.
HC 20
see plate 119

JASPER JOHNS
Winter, 1989
intaglio from one copper plate,
26 3/4 x 19 1/2 IN.
HC 20
see plate 120

JASPER JOHNS
Untitled, 1991
intaglio from three copper plates,
42 1/2 x 78 IN.
Edition 38, AP 11, pp 3
see plate 141

JASPER JOHNS
Untitled (Primaries with Secondaries),
1991
intaglio from three copper plates,
42 1/2 x 78 IN.
TP 2
see plate 140

JASPER JOHNS
Untitled, 1992
intaglio from seven copper plates,
43 1/2 x 52 1/2 IN.
Edition 50, AP 15, pp 2
see plate 150

JASPER JOHNS
After Holbein, 1994
lithograph from eight
aluminum plates,
32 1/4 x 25 IN.
Edition 42, AP 9, pp 4
see plate 166

JASPER JOHNS
Untitled, 1995
lithograph from five
aluminum plates,
41 3/8 x 53 1/4 IN.
Edition 49, AP 11, pp 5
Jo Fielder, see plate 167

JASPER JOHNS
Untitled, 1995
mezzotint from two copper plates,
26 x 19 IN.
Edition 39, AP 10, pp 2
see plate 168

JASPER JOHNS
Untitled, 1995
mezzotint with drypoint, from
two copper plates
29 3/4 x 22 1/2 IN.
Edition 48, AP 10, pp 1
see plate 169

JASPER JOHNS
Untitled, 1995
mezzotint from two copper plates,
26 x 19 IN.
Edition 37, AP 9, pp 2
see plate 170

JASPER JOHNS
Face with Watch, 1996
intaglio from six copper plates,
42 x 31 7/8 IN.
Edition 50, AP 12, pp 4
see plate 177

JULIAN LETHBRIDGE
B. 1947
Born in Sri Lanka, but primarily raised in England, Julian
Lethbridge studied at West-
chester College and Cambridge
University (1960-1969). Upon
graduation, he began a career as
a banker, but by 1972 he had
moved to New York to paint
and draw. His first exhibition of
paintings and drawings at Julian
Pretto Gallery (1988) was followed within the next year by
one-person exhibitions at Paula
Cooper Gallery in New York
and Daniel Weinberg Gallery in
San Francisco.

Lethbridge's abstraction is
cerebral, often based on mathematical or natural principles.
Methodically building up his
surfaces with pigment, he then
incises them with repeated pat-
terns. In the late 1980s and early
1990s Lethbridge limited his

work to shades of black-and-white, mining the richness of monochromatic painting; more recently he has begun to introduce vibrant colors and more gestural brushwork into his paintings. Lethbridge began printing at ULAE at the suggestion of Bill Goldston in 1989. He has since produced eleven published editions.

JULIAN LETHBRIDGE
Untitled, 1990
lithograph from one aluminum plate,
22 3/4 x 17 IN.
Edition 58, AP 10, pp 3
see plate 131

JULIAN LETHBRIDGE
Untitled, 1991
intaglio from one copper plate,
21 1/2 x 17 IN.
Edition 18, AP 7, pp 2
see plate 142

JULIAN LETHBRIDGE
Access, 1992
lithograph from three aluminum plates and silkscreen from two screens,
26 3/8 x 19 1/4 IN.
Edition 50, AP 12, pp 3
see plate 152

JULIAN LETHBRIDGE
Chapel, 1993
lithograph from two aluminum plates,
51 3/8 x 39 1/2 IN.
Edition 40, AP 8, pp 2
see plate 155

JULIAN LETHBRIDGE
Traveling Salesman, 1995
lithograph from four aluminum plates,
43 3/4 x 42 IN.
Edition 50, AP 9, pp 3
see plate 173

JULIAN LETHBRIDGE
Traveling Salesman, 1995
lithograph from four aluminum plates,
43 3/4 x 42 1/4 IN.
Edition 30, AP 5, pp 2
see plate 172

JULIAN LETHBRIDGE
Untitled, 1995
lithograph from seven aluminum plates,
33 1/4 x 27 IN.
Edition 45, AP 16, pp 3
Doug and Cathleen Bennett,
see plate 171

ALEXANDER LIBERMAN
B. 1912

Alexander Liberman was born in Kiev, Russia to wealthy parents, and received a wide-ranging education that included studies in English, carpentry, and photography. After his family moved to Paris in 1924, he attended the École des Roches, where he studied metal working and history before exploring mathematics and philosophy at the Sorbonne. Fleeing Paris with his family after the German invasion, he settled in New York, where he simultaneously encompassed successful careers in the arts and in publishing. Beginning as a photographer for *Vogue* magazine in 1941, Liberman went on to become artistic director for Condé Nast Publications.

He has always pursued abstraction, but his approach has varied stylistically between a hard-edged style in the 1950s to a more painterly approach in the 1960s and 1970s. He displayed his work in one-person shows at the Museum of Modern Art (1959), Betty Parsons Gallery (1960), and André Emmerich Gallery (1967). A retrospective of his work was organized by the

Corcoran Gallery of Art (1970). Tatyana Grosman invited Liberman to print at ULAE in 1976, during a dinner party in honor of the Russian poet Andrei Voznesensky. Mrs. Grosman suggested that Liberman and Voznesensky collaborate; the resulting unbound book, *Nostalgia for the Present,* 1977-79, consists of seventeen lithographs with the drips, scribbles and scrawls that define Liberman's gestural style.

ALEXANDER LIBERMAN AND
ANDREI VOZNESENSKY
Nostalgia for the Present, 1977-79
17 lithographs from 13 stones and 15 aluminum plates,
each sheet 40 3/4 x 27 1/4 IN.
Unbound book with poem in Russian by Andrei Voznesensky, title, translation and colophon pages in a wood box with a lithograph on the cover.
Edition 28, AP 6, pp 2
see plate 65

MARISOL
B. 1930

Of Venezuelan decent, Marisol was born in Paris, attended high school in Los Angeles, studied for a year in Paris at the École des Beaux Arts and the Académie Julien before moving to New York in 1950 to study painting with Yasuo Kuniyoshi at the Art Students League.

In 1951 she moved to Provincetown, Massachusetts to study with Hans Hofmann until 1954. In 1953 she devoted herself to sculpture, making terracotta figurines, carving figures from wood, and creating assemblages incorporating found objects and plaster castings of her own face. Because her work combined social satire and descriptive realism, it was initially linked to pop art. Marisol's work was included

in the Museum of Modern Art's *The Art of Assemblage* (1961), the Haags Gemeentemuscum's *New Realism* (1964), and the Whitney Museum of American Art's *Annual Exhibition* (1964); in 1968 she represented Venezuela at the Venice *Biennale.*

At the suggestion of Larry Rivers, Marisol began working at ULAE in 1964, and by the following year had completed five lithographs juxtaposing tracings of the artist's hands and feet with outlines of distinctive feminine objects, such as a purse or high-heeled shoes. Between 1970-1973 she produced a body of work based on her extended travels to Asia, Micronesia, and Polynesia, frequently incorporating unorthodox materials into her prints.

MARISOL
Pappagallo, 1965
lithograph from three stones,
25 5/8 x 19 IN.
Edition 20, AP 1
see plate 20

MARISOL
Diptych, 1971
lithograph from two stones,
95 1/2 x 31 5/8 IN.
Edition 33
see plate 43

MARISOL
Catalpa Maiden About to Touch Herself, 1973
lithograph from four stones and one aluminum plate,
40 1/4 x 27 3/4 IN.
Edition 24, AP 4, pp 2
see plate 49

SUZANNE McCLELLAND
B. 1959

Suzanne McClelland earned her BFA at the University of Michigan in 1981; moving to New York, she received an MFA at the School of Visual Arts in 1989. Her first one-person exhibition was with Stephanie Theodore Gallery (1992). She quickly received national attention after her inclusion in the Whitney Museum of American Art's *Biennial Exhibition* (1993) and a site-specific installation for the Whitney's Philip Morris branch.

McClelland wrote in her journals for a number of years before exhibiting, and a sense of writing pervades her style, which explores the relationship between the appearance of words and their meaning. As a result, McClelland's work can be "read" on many levels. Her, splashes, scrawls, and thick blobs of paint or clay allude to the energetic strokes of Jackson Pollock or Willem de Kooning, while her obsessive repetition of a single word creates a highly personal poetry about the shifting, often elusive nature of meaning.

SUZANNE McCLELLAND
Then, 1993
lithograph from six aluminum plates and silkscreen from one screen,
22 X 30 IN.
Edition 55, AP 11, pp 4
see plate 157

SUZANNE McCLELLAND
3:00, 6:00, 9:00, 12:00, 1996
four lithographs from two aluminum plates and silkscreens from a total of 17 screens,
each sheet 47 1/4 X 31 1/2 IN.
Edition 35, AP 4, pp 3
see plates 184, 185, 186, 187

SUZANNE McCLELLAND
Tea Leaves, 1996
lithograph from fifteen aluminum plates and silkscreen from 16 screens with collage,
86 X 108 IN.
Edition 20, AP 6, pp 4
Scott Smith, see plate 181

ROBERT MOTHERWELL
1915-1994

Robert Motherwell studied art and philosophy in Los Angeles and San Francisco before entering Harvard. Interspersing trips to Europe (1932 and 1938-1940) with his studies, he combined graduate studies in philosophy at Harvard with courses in art history at Columbia University in New York. There Motherwell met a number of European Surrealists in exile; he adopted many of their ideas, particularly the notion of automatic writing as a means of tapping into the subconscious. Motherwell also experimented early and often with collage, becoming a widely acknowledged master in this modernist medium.

In the 1950s he began what became his most extensive painting series, *Elegies to the Spanish Republic*. Motherwell first exhibited at Peggy Guggenheim's Art of This Century Gallery (1944). Along with Barnett Newman, Motherwell is the only other abstract expressionist to explore printmaking seriously. After numerous invitations from Tatyana Grosman, he first visited ULAE in 1961 because of the encouragement of his wife, Helen Frankenthaler, who was printing there. Motherwell was a prolific printmaker; creating seventeen editions at ULAE between 1961-1971. While these represent only a fraction of his output as a

printer, they reveal the full range of his interests – from collage, to gestural color to collaborations between artists and poets.

ROBERT MOTHERWELL
Poet I, 1961-62
lithograph from one stone,
30 X 22 1/8 IN.
Edition 22, AP 2
Douglas and Leslie Volle, see plate 7

ROBERT MOTHERWELL
AND RAFAEL ALBERTI
A la pintura, 1968-72
21 intaglios from 38 copper plates,
each sheet 25 3/4 X 38 1/8 IN.
Unbound book of 24 pages with preface by Rafael Alberti, and frontispiece, title, table of contents, end and colophon pages; text is excerpted from *Selected Poems* by Alberti, in a wood and Plexiglas box designed by the artist.
Edition 40, AP 8, pp 2
Renie and Stan Helfgott, see plate 48

ROBERT MOTHERWELL
Samurai, 1971
lithograph from one aluminum plate,
72 5/8 X 36 7/8 IN.
Edition 16
see plate 44

ELIZABETH MURRAY
B. 1940

After earning a BFA from the the School of The Art Institute of Chicago (1962) and an MFA from Mills College in Oakland, California (1964), Elizabeth Murray settled in New York in 1967. Keeping with the spirit of the time, she abandoned painting in favor of interdisciplinary and multimedia works. In 1971, however, Murray resumed painting, and by 1976 had received her first one-person exhibition in New York at Paula Cooper Gallery. By the early 1980s Murray had become well known

for her ability to transform cannily abstracted images of common domestic items – coffee cups, tables, musical instruments, and dogs – into lushly painted, animated low relief forms. Breaking with her early minimalist influences, Murray defined her own particular brand of representation as a balance between illusionistic painting and dimensional sculpture.

Her work has been included in several of the Whitney Museum of American Art's *Biennial Exhibitions* (1973, 1979, and 1985); a survey of her paintings and drawings was organized by the Dallas Museum of Art (1987), and a retrospective of her prints toured to museums throughout the United States and Japan (1990). Murray began printing with ULAE in 1985 on the invitation of Bill Goldston. Initially she turned to lithography as the closest approximation of her drawings, but a collaboration with the poet Anne Waldman combined lithography and etching. By the 1990s she was working with ULAE staff to create prints which incorporate three-dimensional attributes to approximate closely the contours of her increasingly sculptural paintings.

ELIZABETH MURRAY
#1, 1986
lithograph from 13 stones,
22 X 31 IN.
Edition 59, AP 12, pp 2
Douglas and Leslie Volle, see plate 90

ELIZABETH MURRAY
Blue Body, 1986-87
lithograph from two stones and 13 aluminum plates,
47 3/4 X 31 5/8 IN.
Edition 70, AP 12, pp 2
see plate 105

ELIZABETH MURRAY
Up Dog, 1987-88
lithograph from one stone,
12 aluminum plates and two
aluminum plate collages,
45 1/2 x 46 1/2 IN.
Edition 62, AP 7, pp 3
see plate 110

ELIZABETH MURRAY
Down Dog, 1988
lithograph from 14 aluminum
plates and two aluminum
plate collages,
50 3/4 x 41 IN.
Edition 65, AP 12, pp 3
see plate 111

ELIZABETH MURRAY AND ANNE
WALDMAN
Her Story, 1988-90
13 lithographs from 39
aluminum plates with intaglio
from 29 copper plates,
each sheet 11 3/8 x 17 3/4 IN.
Unbound book with title/col-
ophon page and 13 poems by Anne
Waldman in a box.
Edition 74, AP 13, pp 5
see plate 132

ELIZABETH MURRAY
Undoing, 1989-90
lithograph from five aluminum
plates and intaglio from four
copper plates,
29 x 23 IN.
Edition 60, AP 6, pp 3
see plate 133

ELIZABETH MURRAY
Hat, 1991
monotype over intaglio from
two copper plates,
13 1/2 x 10 1/4 IN.
Edition 23
see plate 143

ELIZABETH MURRAY
Wiggle Manhattan, 1992
lithograph from 18
aluminum plates,
58 3/4 x 29 IN.
Edition 47, AP 10, pp 4
Lorena and James Salcedo-Watson,
see plate 153

ELIZABETH MURRAY
Shoe String, 1993
three dimensional lithograph from
36 aluminum plates,
40 3/4 x 33 3/4 x 5 IN.
Edition 70, AP 6, pp 4
see plate 158

ELIZABETH MURRAY
Shack, 1994
three-dimensional lithograph from
143 aluminum plates,
63 x 51 x 3 IN.
Edition 60, AP 15, pp 3
see plate 162

ELIZABETH MURRAY
Lovers, 1996
mezzotint from one copper
plate over monotype from
one plastic plate,
28 3/4 x 26 1/2 IN.
Edition 18, AP 6, pp 2
see plate 176

BARNETT NEWMAN
1905-1970

Barnett Newman studied at the
Art Students League for much of
the 1920s. Shortly after the
beginning of World War II, he
stopped painting and destroyed
his early paintings. He resumed
his search for what he termed
"the tragic and timeless" in 1948;
by the time of his first one-person exhibition at Betty Parsons
Gallery (1950) he was forty-five
years old. Newman used scale
(his 1951 painting *Cathedra* is
eighteen feet long) and sensual
color to create pictorial en-
velopes that could overwhelm
and transform the viewer.

Of all the abstract expressionists, only Newman and
Robert Motherwell seriously
explored printmaking, and both
worked at ULAE. Newman
viewed printmaking as a series
of challenges. Not only did the
relatively small size of lithographic stones require a substan-
tial adjustment from his grandly

scaled canvases, but he initially
found it difficult to achieve his
trademark sense of floating
luminosity via ink-on-paper. In
18 Cantos, 1963-64, he succeeded by exploiting accidents that
occurred during the printmaking process, and by taking
advantage of the way the margins of a sheet of paper naturally
divided space. Newman's respect
for lithography is evident in his
preface to *18 Cantos.* "For me, it
[lithography]…is like a piano or
an orchestra, and as with an
instrument, it interprets. And as
in all the interpretive arts, so in
lithography, creation is joined
with the 'playing;' in this case
not of bow and string, but of
stone and press."

BARNETT NEWMAN
18 Cantos, 1963-64
18 lithographs from seven stones,
sheet size varies from 16 1/2 x
12 3/4 to 25 1/4 x 19 3/4 IN.
Portfolio in a box, designed by the
artist, bound in vellum embossed
with the initials BN.
Edition 18, AP 6
Robert and Jane Meyerhoff, Phoenix,
Maryland, see plate 16

BARNETT NEWMAN
Notes, 1968
18 intaglios from 12 copper plates,
each sheet 19 7/8 x 14 IN.
Portfolio in a box, designed by the
artist, bound in vellum embossed
with the initials BN.
Edition 7, AP 2
Jasper Johns, see plate 37

CLAES OLDENBURG
B. 1929

Born in Stockholm, Claes
Oldenburg immigrated to the
United States with his family in
1936. After graduating from Yale
University (1952), he attended
the School of The Art Institute
of Chicago (1952-1954). Moving
to New York in 1956, he began

creating environments and happenings. In 1960 he created an
environment for the Judson
Gallery called *The Street* which
featured materials he had sal-
vaged from the street over several years. Oldenburg's second
environment, *The Store,* 1961,
was created in his studio, and it
featured painted plaster sculptures of mundane consumer
objects. The following year
Oldenburg began to create the
large soft sculptures for which
he is best known. Retrospective
exhibitions were organized by
the Museum of Modern Art
(1969) and the Los Angeles
Museum of Contemporary Art
(1995); in addition, the artist has
created numerous monumental
outdoor sculptures. Oldenburg
is a skilled draftsman capable of a
keen ironic wit, and he has created a number of notable prints
and multiples. Oldenburg published one print with ULAE.

CLAES OLDENBURG
Tea Pot, 1975
lithograph from one stone,
18 1/4 x 26 1/4 IN.
Edition 34, AP 5, pp 2
see plate 61

ROBERT RAUSCHENBERG
B. 1925

Robert Rauschenberg attended
the Kansas City Art Institute
(1947-1948) and Académie Julien
in Paris (1948) before traveling to
North Carolina to study at Black
Mountain College with Joseph
Albers (1948-1949). While at
Black Mountain College he met
and was strongly influenced by
the interdisciplinary approaches
of fellow students John Cage,
Merce Cunningham, and David
Tudor. Moving to New York in
1949, Rauschenberg studied at
the Art Students League (1949-

1952); in 1953 he met Jasper Johns, initiating a long and productive creative friendship.

Retrospective or survey exhibitions of his art have been organized by many museums, including Amsterdam's Stedelijk Museum (1968), the Smithsonian Institution (1976), the Menil Collection (1991), and the National Gallery of Art (1991). Throughout his career Rauschenberg has embraced technological, conceptual, or stylistic innovation. His works in a wide number of static and performance-based media have been widely exhibited.

In late 1960, Tatyana Grosman met Rauschenberg while delivering stones to Jasper Johns. In April 1962, Rauschenberg went to West Islip and completed seven lithographs that year, including *License*. Throughout his career at ULAE, Rauschenberg has continually set new standards and broken the barriers of modern printmaking. His restless energy and inspiration from events have taken him to over thirty countries and such studios as Gemini G.E.L., GraphicStudio. Styria Studio, Saff Tech Arts as well as his own studio, United Press. His work at ULAE and all of the other studios has resulted in over 750 editions.

ROBERT RAUSCHENBERG
License, 1962
lithograph from four stones,
41 1/4 x 29 1/2 IN.
Edition 16, AP 4
Renie and Stan Helfgott, see plate 8

ROBERT RAUSCHENBERG
Accident, 1963
lithograph from two stones,
41 1/4 x 29 1/2 IN.
Edition 29, AP 4
Lent by the artist, see plate 12

ROBERT RAUSCHENBERG
Breakthrough II, 1965
lithograph from four stones,
48 3/8 x 34 IN.
Edition 34, AP unknown
Renie and Stan Helfgott, see plate 21

ROBERT RAUSCHENBERG
Water Stop, 1968
lithograph from nine stones and intaglio from one copper plate,
54 1/8 x 31 5/8 IN.
Edition 28, AP 4, pp 3
The Schweber Family, see plate 38

ROBERT RAUSCHENBERG
Kitty Hawk, 1974
lithograph from eight stones,
78 5/8 x 40 1/8 IN.
Edition 28, AP 5, pp 2
see plate 54

ROBERT RAUSCHENBERG
Tanya, 1974
lithograph from three stones with embossing,
22 1/2 x 15 3/8 IN.
Edition 50, AP 5, pp 1
see plate 55

ROBERT RAUSCHENBERG
Bellini #1, 1986
intaglio from 11 copper plates,
58 1/4 x 38 1/4 IN.
Edition 36, AP 6, pp 2
see plate 91

ROBERT RAUSCHENBERG
Bellini #2, 1987
intaglio from eight copper plates,
58 7/8 x 37 1/4 IN.
Edition 48, AP 8, pp 3
see plate 92

ROBERT RAUSCHENBERG
Bellini #3, 1988
intaglio from 12 copper plates,
59 x 37 1/2 IN.
Edition 49, AP 8, pp 5
see plate 93

ROBERT RAUSCHENBERG
Bellini #4, 1988
intaglio from 11 copper plates,
60 x 38 1/2 IN.
Edition 47, AP 5, pp 4
see plate 94

ROBERT RAUSCHENBERG
Bellini #5, 1989
intaglio from ten copper plates,
59 x 38 1/4 IN.
Edition 50, AP 9, pp 5
see plate 95

ROBERT RAUSCHENBERG
Soviet/American Array I, 1988-89
intaglio from 14 copper plates,
88 1/2 x 53 1/2 IN.
Edition 55, AP 11, pp 6
see plate 121

ROBERT RAUSCHENBERG
Soviet/American Array II, 1988-90
intaglio from 14 copper plates,
87 3/4 x 52 1/4 IN.
Edition 55, AP 11, pp 5
see plate 122

ROBERT RAUSCHENBERG
Soviet/American Array III, 1989-90
intaglio from nine copper plates,
87 3/4 x 52 1/4 IN.
Edition 57, AP 14, pp 3
see plate 123

ROBERT RAUSCHENBERG
Soviet/American Array IV, 1988-90
intaglio from eight copper plates,
88 1/2 x 52 IN.
Edition 58, AP 13, pp 3
see plate 124

ROBERT RAUSCHENBERG
Soviet/American Array V, 1988-90
intaglio from ten copper plates,
88 1/2 x 53 1/2 IN.
Edition 55, AP 13, pp 2
see plate 125

ROBERT RAUSCHENBERG
Street Sounds, 1992
intaglio from 28 copper plates with photogravure and collage,
46 x 55 IN.
Edition 38, AP 10, pp 6
see plate 151

ROBERT RAUSCHENBERG
Ground Rules (Intermission), 1996
intaglio from from six copper plates,
63 x 51 3/4 IN.
Edition 44, AP 9, pp 5
see plate 188

ROBERT RAUSCHENBERG
Ground Rules (Banco), 1996
intaglio from from six copper plates,
41 3/8 x 27 1/2 IN.
Edition 44, AP 10, pp 5
see plate 189

LARRY RIVERS
B. 1923
Larry Rivers studied musical composition at the Juilliard School of Music (1944-1945) before attending Hans Hofmann's school in Provincetown, Massachusetts (1947-1948). Returning to New York, he graduated from New York University (1951) after studying with William Baziotes. But despite the influence of these two proponents of abstraction, he developed his own distinctive brand of figurative realism that is often associated with pop art. Rivers received his first one-person exhibition at the Jane Street Gallery (1949); along with Grace Hartigan, he was selected by Clement Greenberg and Meyer Schapiro for inclusion in *Talent: 1950* at Kootz Gallery.

Rivers was the first artist invited to work at ULAE; when he arrived in 1957, the minimal working conditions included a single press and part-time printers. His first project, with the poet Frank O'Hara, entitled *Stones,* 1957-1960, fulfilled Tatyana Grosman's goal of encouraging artists and writers to collaborate in the studio. Subsequent prints, such as *French Money,* 1963 and *Lucky Strike II,* 1963 show Rivers developing the historically allusive figuration for which he is best known. As Rivers' sophistication as a printmaker developed, so did the technical abilities of

ULAE's facility and staff; and the artist expanded his prints to include sculptural constructions in the three-dimensional lithograph *Diana with Poem*, 1970-74. In 1967 Rivers began a collaboration with the writer Terry Southern. *The Donkey and the Darling,* 1967-77 is a complex book of fifty-two lithographs that took ten years to complete. In 1983 Rivers completed the eleven-color lithograph *Garbo Grosman* as a posthumous tribute to Tatyana.

LARRY RIVERS AND FRANK O'HARA
Stones, 1957-60
12 lithographs from 12 stones,
19 x 23 1/4 IN.
Portfolio with title and colophon pages in a cloth folder in a screen-printed cardboard folder, in a wood box.
Edition 25, AP 5
see plate 1

LARRY RIVERS
Jack of Spades, 1960
lithograph from six stones,
42 3/8 x 30 IN.
Edition 35, AP 1
Lent by the artist, see plate 4

LARRY RIVERS
Lucky Strike II, 1960-63
lithograph from three stones,
29 5/8 x 20 3/4 IN.
Edition 29, AP 2
see plate 14

LARRY RIVERS
French Money, 1963
lithograph from ten stones,
22 1/2 x 31 1/2 IN.
Edition 32 AP unknown
The National Gallery of Art, Washington, Gift of the Woodward Foundation, Washington DC 1976.56.160
see plate 13

LARRY RIVERS AND TERRY SOUTHERN
The Donkey and the Darling, 1967-77
52 lithographs from 166 stones and 334 aluminum plates, each sheet 18 1/2 x 24 1/2 IN.
Unbound book with cover, title, dedication, table of contents, and colophon pages in a wood box with hand-blown glass inset.
Edition 35
see plate 64

LARRY RIVERS AND KENNETH KOCH
Diana with Poem, 1970-74
three-dimensional lithograph from seven stones and one aluminum plate,
22 5/8 x 26 5/8 IN.
Bound with a poem by Kenneth Koch in a linen folder, which when raised forms a box.
Edition 19, AP 7
see plate 56

LARRY RIVERS
For Adults Only, 1971
diptych lithograph from three stones, six aluminum plates and two stencils,
70 1/2 x 29 1/2 IN.
Edition 35, AP 4, pp 3
see plate 45

LARRY RIVERS
Garbo Grosman, 1983
lithograph from 13 stones and one aluminum plate,
31 x 36 IN.
The paper was made in honor of Tatyana Grosman and the color of the paper was named "Tatyana."
Edition 38, AP 7, pp 4
see plate 74

JAMES ROSENQUIST
B. 1933
James Rosenquist attended the Minneapolis School of Art (1948) and studied at the University of Minnesota (1952-1954) before moving to New York, where he studied at the Art Students League and attended drawing classes organized by Jack Youngerman and Robert Indiana (1957-1958). Rosenquist supported himself for much of the 1950s by working as a billboard painter, first with the General Outdoor Advertising Company in Minneapolis, and later for the ArtKraft Straus Billboard Company in New York. This experience was instrumental to his artistic development, and smoothly painted, vibrantly colored, large-scale images of consumer items, movie stars, and random elements of popular culture became the subjects of his painting. In 1962 Rosenquist was included in the Sidney Janis Gallery's *New Talent* show, and received a one-person exhibition at the Green Gallery. His work was exhibited internationally throughout the 1960s, and was included in the exhibition of pop art at Amsterdam's Stedelijk Museum (1964), the São Paulo *Biennale* (1967), the Whitney Museum of American Art's *Annual Exhibition* (1967), and *Documenta 4* (1968); in 1972 the Whitney Museum of American Art organized a survey of his paintings and in 1985 the Denver Art Museum presented a paintings retrospective that also travelled to Houston, Des Moines, Buffalo and Washington, DC.

Tatyana Grosman first saw Rosenquist's work at his 1962 Green Gallery exhibition, and, with the help of Jasper Johns, brought him to ULAE, where he worked from 1964-1987.

JAMES ROSENQUIST
Spaghetti and Grass, 1964-65
lithograph from five stones,
31 1/4 x 22 1/4 IN.
Edition 23, AP 2
Fearer Family Collection, see plate 23

JAMES ROSENQUIST
Campaign, 1965
lithograph from four stones,
29 3/8 x 22 3/8 IN.
Edition 26, AP 1
see plate 22

JAMES ROSENQUIST
Circles of Confusion I, 1965-66
lithograph from four stones,
38 3/8 x 28 IN.
Edition 12, AP 8
Personal Collection of Leo Castelli, New York, see plate 28

JAMES ROSENQUIST
Expo 67 Mural - Firepole 33' x 17', 1967
lithograph from six stones,
34 x 18 7/8 IN.
Edition 41, AP 5, pp 2
see plate 29

JAMES ROSENQUIST
Off the Continental Divide, 1973-74
lithograph from 29 aluminum plates,
43 x 79 1/8 IN.
Edition 43, AP 5, pp 2
see plate 57

JAMES ROSENQUIST
Chambers, 1980
lithograph from 16 aluminum plates,
30 x 47 1/8 IN.
Edition 45, AP 11, pp 3
Mr. and Mrs. Dennis Kannenberg, see plate 67

JAMES ROSENQUIST
Dog Descending a Staircase, 1980-82
lithograph from one stone and ten aluminum plates and intaglio from one copper plate,
42 x 70 IN.
Edition 33, AP 5, pp 4
see plate 72

JAMES ROSENQUIST
Electrical Nymphs on a Non-Objective Ground, 1984
lithograph from 16 aluminum plates,
42 x 42 IN.
Edition 30, AP 10, pp 5
see plate 79

JAMES ROSENQUIST
The Persistence of Electrons in Space,
1987
intaglio from six copper plates,
40 x 36 5/8 IN.
Edition 48, AP 8, pp 4
Craig and Lisa Zammiello,
see plate 104

SUSAN ROTHENBERG
B. 1945
Susan Rothenberg attended Cornell University until the head of the department discouraged her from studying sculpture. She lived abroad for a year before returning to complete her undergraduate studies in 1967. After briefly attending the Corcoran School of Art, she moved to New York in 1969, where she continued sculptural experiments and began to paint minimalist-inspired geometric grids. In 1973 Rothenberg's frustration with such minimalist issues as flatness and anti-illusionism produced the first of the horse paintings for which the artist became well known.

While her first exhibitions of these expressive, painterly, and psychologically-charged iconic images were coolly received, by 1978, when she was included in the Whitney Museum of American Art's *New Image Painting,* her unique blend of abstraction and representation was seen as the herald of a resurgence in painting. In 1980 Rothenberg was included in the American pavilion of the Venice *Biennale;* in 1982 she was the subject of a one-person exhibition at the Stedelijk Museum, Amsterdam, and was the only woman included in the influential *Zeitgeist* exhibition in West Berlin. Traveling surveys of her work have been organized by the Los Angeles

County Museum of Art (1983) and the Albright-Knox Art Gallery (1994). Bill Goldston invited Rothenbeg to work at ULAE after seeing her paintings in the Whitney Museum of American Art's 1983 *Biennial Exhibition.* Rothenberg has produced print images using woodcut and mezzotint techniques.

SUSAN ROTHENBERG
Between the Eyes, 1983-84
lithograph from one stone and woodcut from one woodblock with collage,
57 1/2 x 34 IN.
Edition 36, AP 6, pp 2
see plate 76

SUSAN ROTHENBERG
Plug, 1983
lithograph from three stones,
30 x 22 IN.
Edition 29, AP 5, pp 3
see plate 75

SUSAN ROTHENBERG
Four Green Lines, 1984
lithograph from three stones and one aluminum plate,
30 1/2 x 35 IN.
Edition 30, AP 5, pp 2
see plate 77

SUSAN ROTHENBERG
Missing Corners, 1984
monoprint from one woodblock,
24 x 15 1/2 IN.
Edition 18
see plate 78

SUSAN ROTHENBERG
Stumblebum, 1985-86
lithograph from two stones and 15 aluminum plates,
86 1/2 x 42 1/2 IN.
Edition 40, AP 8, pp 2
see plate 97

SUSAN ROTHENBERG
Blue Violin, 1986
woodcut from six woodblocks,
65 x 42 1/2 IN.
Edition 37, AP 5, pp 2
Laura Burrows-Jackson, Baltimore, Maryland, see plate 96

SUSAN ROTHENBERG
Fish Sculpture, 1987
aluminum filled epoxy resin mounted on granite block,
fish: 12 1/4 x 3 x 2 IN.,
base: 8 1/2 x 5 x 5 IN.
Edition 11, AP 5
see plate 106

SUSAN ROTHENBERG
Listening Bamboo, 1989-90
woodcut from one woodblock,
54 1/4 x 83 1/2 IN.
Edition 23, AP 8, pp 1
see plate 134

SUSAN ROTHENBERG
Mezzo Fist #1, 1990
mezzotint from one copper plate with collage,
31 x 22 1/2 IN.
Edition 49, AP 10, pp 4
see plate 135

EDWIN SCHLOSSBERG
B. 1945
Edwin Schlossberg was introduced to Tatyana Grosman in the summer of 1967 by their mutual friend Jasper Johns. At this time, Schlossberg, a devotee of the teachings of R. Buckminster Fuller, was studying linguistics, physics, and literature at Columbia University.

Mrs. Grosman, who was always searching for ways to combine art and literature, invited the young poet to print at ULAE. Schlossberg was then making his own books, using unorthodox materials such as aluminum foil and plastic wrap. His first and most significant project at ULAE, *WORDS-WORDSWORDS* 1967-68, consists of seventeen poems that examine how the presentation of words can change their meaning. Using different typefaces ranging from large, crudely rendered stencil to typewriter Elite, Schlossberg's poems are printed on a wide variety of

materials, including Plexiglas, aluminum foil, and paper. Taking full advantage of the techniques then available at ULAE, Schlossberg employed embossing, blind embossing, lithography, letterpress, and etching to complete his project. All seventeen pages with colophon page and a preface by Robert Rauschenberg are contained in a handmade aluminum box. Schlossberg completed two other projects for ULAE, *Fragments from a Place,* 1974, and a series of prints in 1981 that incorporated the newly developed temperature-sensitive material Liquid Crystal as a color medium.

EDWIN SCHLOSSBERG
WORDSWORDSWORDS,
1967-68
Medium varies but includes lithographs from stones, intaglios from copper plates, and embossing,
each sheet 11 x 8 1/2 IN.
Unbound book of 17 poems with a preface by Robert Rauschenberg, title and colophon pages, in a paper folder in an aluminum box.
Edition 25
Robert and Brenda Edelson,
see plate 39

EDWIN SCHLOSSBERG
Edges Strengthen, 1981
lithograph from two stones in Liquid Crystal,
41 7/8 x 29 5/8 IN.
Edition 23, pp 2
see plate 68

EDWIN SCHLOSSBERG
Warm Memories, 1981
lithograph from one stone,
19 1/8 x 25 3/4 IN.
Edition 21, pp 2
see plate 69

JOEL SHAPIRO
B. 1941

Joel Shapiro received his undergraduate and graduate degrees from New York University (1961-1969). He had his first one-person museum exhibition at the Museum of Contemporary Art, Chicago (1976), and was included in the Whitney Museum of American Art's *Biennial Exhibition* (1981), *Documenta 7* (1982), and the Carnegie Museum of Art's *International* (1988).

In the 1990s, Shapiro completed a number of monumentally-scaled public sculpture, including a commission for the Holocaust Museum in Washington, DC. In the early 1970s Shapiro began making sculptures that extended the stylistic ideals and conceptual ideas of minimalism, but by the mid 1970s began to develop the planar, largely geometric figurative and architectural references for which he is best known. Shapiro's oeuvre also consists of a significant production of drawings and prints. He has printed with numerous ateliers, including Simca Press, Grenfell Press, and Aldo Crommelynck. Invited to print at ULAE in 1985, he produced a series of three different but closely related woodcuts. Described by ULAE as "wood collage prints," they incorporate the wood trim of a doll house, inked and printed, to create the print's imagery.

JOEL SHAPIRO
#1, 1985
wood collage
17 X 13 1/2 IN.
Edition 41, AP 8, pp 1
see plate 86

JOEL SHAPIRO
#2, 1985
wood collage
19 X 24 IN.
Edition 44, AP 7, pp 1
see plate 87

JOEL SHAPIRO
#3, 1985
wood collage
17 X 13 1/2 IN.
Edition 41, AP 8, pp 1
see plate 88

KIKI SMITH
B. 1954

Unlike many artists of her generation, Kiki Smith did not study art in an academic setting. Instead, she learned by participating in Collaborative Projects (Colab), a New York-based cooperative that in the mid-1970s featured an active membership of over forty artists. Colab's sociopolitical agenda advocated rebellion against the status quo, organizing unconventional exhibitions featuring collaborative artworks made from inexpensive, often blatantly uncommercial materials. Colab's philosophy of unorthodox methods and materials can be seen in Smith's use of doilies, glitter, string, and construction paper, and in her penchant for craft-oriented processes such as Xerography and sewing.

Smith began by making sculptures and drawings that isolated fluids, veins, skin, bones, sex organs, or hair into self-sufficient fragments. More recently, she has diversified her conceptual and technical approach to figuration, creating life-sized figures in a host of traditional and unconventional materials. Smith received the first of many one-person exhibitions in New York at Fawbush Gallery (1988); in 1990 Smith's work was the focus of the Museum of Modern Art's *Projects* series. Since then, she has exhibited internationally, participating in the Whitney Museum of American Art's *Biennial Exhibition* (1991 and 1993), and has received one-person exhibitions at Geneva's Centre d'Art Contemporaine (1990), Amsterdam's Institute for Contemporary Art (1991), Denmark's Louisiana Museum (1993), and London's Whitechapel Art Gallery (1994). Bill Goldston invited Smith to print at ULAE in 1989, and she has worked in a variety of media including etching, Xerox transfer and mixed media constructions.

KIKI SMITH
Untitled, 1990
lithograph from nine stones and one aluminum plate,
36 X 36 IN.
Edition 54, AP 11, pp 1
see plate 136

KIKI SMITH
Banshee Pearls, 1991
12 lithographs from 51 aluminum plates,
each sheet 22 1/2 X 30 1/2 IN.
Edition 51, AP 12, pp 3
Dr. Robert and Mrs. Lisa Feldman, see plate 145

KIKI SMITH
Sueño, 1992
intaglio from two copper plates,
41 3/4 X 77 1/2 IN.
Edition 33, AP 6, pp 2
see plate 146

KIKI SMITH
Worm, 1992
intaglio from four copper plates with collage,
42 X 62 IN.
Edition 30, AP 10, pp 4
see plate 147

KIKI SMITH
Kiki Smith 1993, 1993
intaglio from two copper plates,
73 X 36 1/2 IN.
Edition 33, AP 10, pp 3
see plate 159

KIKI SMITH
My Blue Lake, 1995
lithograph from one aluminum plate with photogravure from one copper plate,
43 1/2 X 54 3/4 IN.
Edition 41, AP 7, pp 5
John and Christina Lund, see plate 174

SAUL STEINBERG
B. 1914

Born in Romania, Saul Steinberg studied philosophy at the University of Bucharest and architecture at the Polytechnic Institute in Milan. There he contributed cartoons for the magazine *Bertoldo*. Soon after his immigration to New York in 1941, he had drawings published in a number of prestigious magazines, including *The New Yorker* and *PM*. His art, which still appears in *The New Yorker*, has been favorably compared with political satirists such as William Hogarth, Honoré Daumier, and Henri Toulouse-Lautrec.

Steinberg had his first one-person exhibition at New York's Wakefield Gallery (1943), and was included in the Museum of Modern Art's *Fourteen Americans* (1946) and the Whitney Museum of American Art's *Annual Exhibition* (1949). In 1978, the Whitney Museum organized a traveling retrospective of the artist's paintings, drawings, sculptures, and prints. Tatyana Grosman invited Steinberg to print at ULAE in 1972. His first lithographs, *The Museum*, 1972, and *Main Street*, 1972-73, place whimsical characters against bleak backgrounds or in bureaucratic offices. Steinberg's penchant for stamped imagery, which he often incorporated in his drawings, is also present in these lithographs. In *The Museum* embossed images replace framed works of art; in *Main Street* the embossing becomes an iconic substitute for the rising sun.

SAUL STEINBERG
Main Street, 1972-73
lithograph from one stone and one aluminum plate,
22 5/8 x 30 IN.
Edition 40, AP 4, pp 2
John and Christina Lund, see plate 51

SAUL STEINBERG
The Museum, 1972
lithograph from one stone and one aluminum plate,
20 3/4 x 28 1/8 IN.
Edition 34, AP 8
see plate 50

CY TWOMBLY
B. 1928
Cy Twombly studied at the Boston Museum School of Fine Arts (1948-1949) and Washington and Lee University (1949-1950) before attending Black Mountain College (1950-1951), where he studied with Robert Motherwell and Franz Kline. For much of the 1950s Twombly traveled and lived in North Africa, Spain, and Italy; in 1957 he settled in Rome. Today he lives and works both in Europe and Lexington, Virginia.

Twombly's calligraphic abstractions were first shown in New York at Kootz Gallery (1951); since then his paintings have been widely exhibited internationally, appearing in the Venice *Biennale* (1964) and the Whitney Museum of American Art's *Annual* and *Biennial Exhibitions* (1967, 1969, and 1973). Retrospective exhibitions of his art have been organized by the Whitney Museum of American Art (1979) and the Museum of Modern Art (1995). Robert Rauschenberg introduced Twombly to ULAE in the

summer of 1967, inviting him to view a series of lithographs then in progress. This encounter resulted in the creation of a number of prints by Twombly; many of these prints were not editioned until the mid-1970s, largely because of the infrequency of the artist's visits to the United States. Twombly's first ULAE portfolio was *Sketches*, 1967-75, six intimately scaled etchings; his *Note*, 1967 series, which is closer in style to the calligraphic abstraction for which he is best known, also shows Tatyana Grosman's encouraging artists to incorporate unusual, often hand-made, paper as an essential part of their print projects.

CY TWOMBLY
Note I, 1967
intaglio from one copper plate,
25 7/8 x 20 3/8 IN.
Edition 14, AP 4, pp 1, CP
see plate 30

CY TWOMBLY
Note II, 1967
intaglio from one copper plate,
25 1/2 x 20 1/4 IN.
Edition 14, AP 4, pp 1, CP
see plate 31

CY TWOMBLY
Note III, 1967
intaglio from one copper plate,
25 5/8 x 20 3/8 IN.
Edition 14, AP 4, pp 1, CP
see plate 32

CY TWOMBLY
Note IV, 1967
intaglio from one copper plate,
25 3/8 x 20 1/4 IN.
Edition 14, AP 4, pp 1, CP
see plate 33

CY TWOMBLY
Sketches, 1967-75
six intaglios from six copper plates,
each sheet 8 1/2 x 12 1/4 IN.
Portfolio with a title/colophon page in a folder and an envelope.
Edition 18, AP 5, pp 1
Robert Rauschenberg, see plate 60

CY TWOMBLY
Untitled I, 1967, published 1974
intaglio from one copper plate,
27 1/2 x 40 5/8 IN.
Edition 19, AP 5, pp 1
see plate 58

CY TWOMBLY
Untitled II, 1967, published 1974
intaglio from one copper plate,
27 3/8 x 40 3/8 IN.
Edition 23, AP 5, pp 1
Peter and Susan Ralston, see plate 59

TERRY WINTERS
B. 1949
Terry Winters attended the High School of Art and Design in New York, and received a BFA from the Pratt Institute (1971). His early paintings were influenced by the minimalist, monochromatic paintings of Brice Marden. However, Winters' love of drawing and his growing interest in depiction led him to introduce schematic references to biological, astronomical, or architectural structures as the subject of his paintings. By the early 1980s, these had developed into loose grids of organic shapes against lushly painted fields.

Winters' first one-person exhibition in New York was at Sonnabend Gallery (1982); he was subsequently included in the Whitney Museum of American Art's *Biennial Exhibition* (1985, 1987, and 1995) and the Corcoran Gallery of Art's 40th *Biennial Exhibition of Contemporary American Painting* (1987). Survey exhibitions of his art

have been organized by the Los Angeles Museum of Contemporary Art, (1991) and the Whitney Museum of American Art (1991). Bill Goldston invited Winters to print at ULAE in 1982; his first print *Ova*, 1982, shows his affinity for lithographic techniques. As Winters continued to work at ULAE, his prints became increasingly complex, offering a solution between drawing and painting. He was able to achieve the fresh look of greasy drawings and smudges while also constructing layers of images through the use of different plates, At the peak of his lithographic exploration, he created *Folio*, 1986, culminating in 136 plates, 140 printings and 102 colors. Since then he has divided his time between etching and lithography.

TERRY WINTERS
Morula I, 1983-84
lithograph from one stone and three aluminum plates,
41 3/4 x 31 5/8 IN.
Edition 38, AP 5, pp 3
see plate 80

TERRY WINTERS
Morula II, 1983-84
lithograph from three stones and five aluminum plates,
42 1/4 x 32 1/2 IN.
Edition 37, AP 6, pp 3
see plate 81

TERRY WINTERS
Morula III, 1983-84
lithograph from eight aluminum plates,
42 x 32 1/2 IN.
Edition 36, AP 5, pp 3
see plate 82

TERRY WINTERS
Novalis, 1983-89
intaglio from one copper plate,
42 1/2 x 31 IN.
Edition 50, AP 10, pp 3
see plate 127

TERRY WINTERS
Double Standard, 1984
lithograph from 18
aluminum plates,
78 x 42 IN.
Edition 40, AP 8, pp 2
see plate 83

TERRY WINTERS
Folio, 1986
11 lithographs from 136
aluminum plates,
each sheet 31 x 22 1/2 IN.
Portfolio with title and colophon
pages in a box designed by the
artist.
Edition 39, AP 6, pp 2
see plates 98, 190-200

TERRY WINTERS
Marginalia, 1988
lithograph from 17
aluminum plates,
48 x 31 3/4 IN.
Edition 66, AP 8, pp 4
see plate 113

TERRY WINTERS
Fourteen Etchings, 1989
14 intaglios from 27 copper plates,
each sheet 18 5/8 x 14 1/8 IN.
Portfolio with colophon page in a
printed folder in a box.
Edition 65, AP 8, pp 3
see plates 126, 205-217

TERRY WINTERS
Section, 1991
lithograph from three stones
and one aluminum plate,
59 1/2 x 40 IN.
Edition 68, AP 10, pp 2
see plate 144

TERRY WINTERS
Theorem, 1992
lithograph from 18
aluminum plates,
31 3/4 x 48 1/8 IN.
Edition 41, AP 12, pp 2
see plate 154

TERRY WINTERS
Models for Synthetic Pictures, 1994
12 intaglios from 57 copper plates,
each sheet 19 3/8 x 22 1/4 IN.
Portfolio in a box.
Edition 35, AP 9, pp 4
see plates 163, 224-234

TERRY WINTERS
Systems Diagram, 1996
intaglio from one copper plate,
42 x 50 IN.
Edition 18, AP 7, pp 3
see plate 182

TERRY WINTERS
Untitled, 1996
lithograph from 14
aluminum plates,
33 3/4 x 48 IN.
Edition 48, AP 10, pp 3
Bruce and Marlene Wankel,
see plate 183

Photograph Credits and Colophon

Photograph Credits

P. 26 (BOTTOM)
The Art Institute of Chicago

P. 35, PLATE 58
Baltimore Museum of Art, Women's
Committee Fund for Contemporary Prints
BMA 1976.35

PLATE 24
Ediciones Poligrafa

P. 18 (BOTTOM)
Mr. Esterow, The New York Times

P. 26 (TOP)
Roxanna Everett

PP. 14, 15 (BOTTOM),
107, 108, 117, 118, 119, 120
Jo Fielder Photography, © 1990, 1996

P. 27 (BOTTOM)
Bill Goldston, © ULAE 1977

P. 121
Larissa Goldston, © ULAE 1996

PLATE 50
Peter Harholdt

P. 115
John A. Lund, © 1989

PP. 19 (BOTTOM), 20
Ugo Mulas

PLATE 9
The Museum of Modern Art, New York,
Gift of the Celeste and Armand Bartos
Foundation, © 1997

PP. 13, 18 (TOP), 19 (TOP), 21, 24 (TOP AND
BOTTOM), 25 (TOP AND BOTTOM), 26 (CENTER),
105 (TOP)
Hans Namuth, © 1958, 1960, 1962, 1969

PP. 23 (TOP)
R. B. Neilly

PP. 105 (BOTTOM), 106
Bob Petersen

PP. 112
Lorena Salcedo-Watson, © ULAE 1988

PP. 17 (BOTTOM), 27 (TOP)
Harry Shunk, © ULAE 1968

PP. 109, 111, 113, 114
Craig Zammiello, © ULAE 1996

Unless otherwise noted, all illustrations and photographs are courtesy of Universal Limited Art Editions.

This book was designed by Lisa Ratkus, in the graphic design office of the Corcoran Gallery of Art, and typeset and produced on an Apple Macintosh computer. The fonts used, Bembo and Orator, were drawn for the Macintosh by Adobe Systems Incorporated.

5,000 copies of this book were printed by M. Marcisak Printing, Bay Shore, NY.

The cover paper, Taxi Cab Yellow, was custom made by Twinrocker Handmade Paper, Brookston, IN. Additionally, the type was foil stamped in match red and the ULAE chop was single-level, blind embossed, by Eagle Gold Stamping, Farmingdale, NY.

All text pages were printed four color process on Monadnock Dulcet, 100 lb. text in Neutral White. The fly sheet was printed with 3 match colors on Gilbert Gilclear, 28 lb.

All four color images were scanned and separated by Island Litho, Farmingdale, NY.

The book was smyth sewn by HOROWITZ/RAE Book Manufacturing, Inc., Fairfield, NJ.